The Magazine Writer's Handbook

Also by Gordon Wells:

The Craft of Writing Articles
The Successful Author's Handbook
How to Communicate

Other Allison & Busby books about writing:

The Craft of Novel Writing by Dianne Doubtfire
How to Publish your Poetry by Peter Finch

Gordon Wells

THE MAGAZINE WRITER'S HANDBOOK

Allison & Busby
LONDON · NEW YORK

First published 1985 by
Allison & Busby Limited
6a Noel Street, London W1V 3RB
Distributed in the USA by
Schocken Books Inc
62 Cooper Square
New York, NY 10003
Reprinted 1986

British Library Cataloguing in Publication Data

Wells, Gordon
  The magazine writer's handbook.
  1. English periodicals
  I. Title
  070.1'75'0941   PN5118

  ISBN 0-85031-630-8

Set in Times by Falcon Graphic Art Ltd
Wallington, Surrey
Printed and bound in Great Britain by
Richard Clay (The Chaucer Press Ltd)
Bungay, Suffolk

CONTENTS

1
Introduction

Successful writing for magazines depends on three things: a good imagination or a knowledge of a particular subject; an ability to put words together; and a knowledge of where to sell one's work — the market. Putting this in another way, success comes from knowing what to write, how to write it, and who to write it for. This handbook is intended to assist writers in selling their work: to help with the essential study of the market — "who to write it for".

No handbook can obviate the need for writers to study the market themselves. Any handbook such as this is almost bound to be out of date at least in some details before it can be published. Yet some things about the market do not change and this handbook will provide an excellent foundation upon which the writer can build. The wise writer will use it to provide an overall view, a "first sift", of the market-place — a guide towards the magazines that warrant further, more detailed study.

The choice

There are several hundred magazines and newspapers published regularly in Great Britain and many of these accept speculative material submitted by freelance writers. This handbook considers which, to the freelance, are the most interesting of these publications. The choice of publications to feature in this handbook has been based on three considerations — two negative, one positive:

> need for specialized knowledge;
> need for localized knowledge;
> payment for publication.

These considerations have led to the exclusion of all specialist trade, profession or hobby publications — who but a pharmacist could write for *The Pharmaceutical Journal* or an aeromodeller for the *Aeromodeller* magazine? And there are many such publications. Of course, this is not to suggest that a freelance writer should not try writing for such publications as *The Pharmaceutical Journal* — if he or she is a pharmacist by profession. But a pharmacist will probably know the journal well and will not need the "first sift" market study that this handbook offers.

Similarly, any freelance writer based in Sussex will be well aware of the local *Sussex Life* county magazine and be able perhaps to contribute to it. He or she will certainly be less readily able to contribute to *Lancashire Life*. Any freelance who particularly wishes to contribute to a remote county magazine should buy a copy anyway: no handbook will do away with that need.

And, in further justification of the carefully limited scope of this handbook, the reader is reminded of the wisdom of Samuel Johnson, who pointed out that "none but a blockhead" would write without prospect of payment. There is little point in studying a market that will not provide an opportunity of recouping the cost of that study.

The choice of magazines for inclusion in this handbook was based on the considerations listed above. The resultant list can be classified under three headings:

— women's magazines: overall this is the biggest magazine market, particularly for short stories, but also very much for non-fiction work. (There is a tendency though for some of the women's magazines to prefer commissioned non-fiction to unsolicited submissions.)

— general interest magazines: on the whole these tend to be the "countryside" glossies, or those of that ilk — but these are not always the best of payers. Within this category, though, there are some of the more widely read women's magazines too, such as *SHE*, *The Lady*, and *My Weekly*.

— leisure interest magazines: although specialist magazines have been excluded, I have assumed that most writers know at least something about doing things in the house and in the garden — and a bit about writing. It is therefore not unreasonable to include a few such magazines. (And, because many non-fiction writers also illustrate their work, the biggest weekly photographic magazine has been included.)

Some of the publications investigated in detail in this handbook accept no fiction, others accept no non-fiction. All of those examined accept either fiction or non-fiction submitted speculatively by freelance writers without editorial "pull" or the benefit of a famous name: "ordinary" spare-time writers like us. The reports included in the handbook are all based on own study; they are not just editors' "blurbs". Each of the study reports have however been submitted to the relevant editor and then corrected, where necessary. (Not all editors responded.)

Payment

One of the most important things for a freelance to know about a magazine is how much the editor will pay for a writer's work. It is not enough to know that the editor pays; is the payment enough? Freelances will wish to decide whether they are prepared to invest the work needed to research and write — and perhaps illustrate too — a feature article for a mere £10, or for a more generous £80, per thousand words. Yet far too many editors still prefer not to disclose this vital — and basic — information to writers in advance.

Payment information has been sought from every magazine listed in this handbook. If the editor would not say what the normal payment rate is, he/she has been asked to at least identify where the payment lies within four broad groups. ("A" £0 – £20; "B" £21 – £40; "C" £41 – £70; and "D" £71 and above — all per 1000 words.) Where the editor has felt unable even to do this, I have made my own assessment of the likely payment group — which could well be wrong, but I know no other figure — and marked this pay-group guess with an asterisk (*).

Readership

In order to sell freelance material to magazines it is important to give the editor what he/she wants. And this can only be done with any confidence if the writer has a clear idea of the magazine's readership. If a magazine is directed at teenage girls, it is almost certainly pointless to try to sell the editor a short story about a grandmother's problems with her grandson. Even if the story were brilliant, the editor would not be interested — because the magazine's readers would not "identify" with the characters.

The easiest way for a freelance to ascertain, with any certainty, the typical reader of any magazine is from the advertisements and readers' letters. Advertising agencies know their media well; they do not advertise their products in a magazine whose readership is not interested in them.

For that reason, the magazine studies in this handbook include an appraisal of the advertisements as well as of the editorial pages. This appraisal is not in terms of A/B/C/D type readership — which means a lot to an advertising man, though little to the average writer — but is in more emotive, meaningful terms. "Up-market" is not a precise term, nor is "home catalogue-shoppers" — but a readership can readily be pictured from such terms. Similarly, the reader's average age is less than precise: advertisers may need this precision, writers do not.

Each of the market study reports includes brief details of a few recent feature articles that the magazine has carried. These are useful in two ways: they indicate the range, or type, of feature that the editor is — or has been — interested in using, and in that sense are a model for future submissions; they also provide the freelance writer with ideas for articles — on similar subjects — that might be offered to other magazines. There need be no worries about plagiarism in "lifting" such article ideas; the end result will inevitably be very different from the original — and we all borrow ideas.

The market study reports also include details of the regular columns carried by the magazine. These are of importance to the freelance writer for the simple reason that the editor is most unlikely to accept a feature article on a subject usually reserved for the columnist — who is probably paid a regular retainer.

Magazine ranking

As well as the details of the requirements of each magazine, it may also be of interest, and some use, to the freelance writer to know which magazines — in my very subjective judgement, which is explained later — are "the best". A magazine that takes a lot of unsolicited material, even though it may not pay as well as some, is often a very worthwhile market for the "ordinary" freelance writer to cultivate. In my ranking of the "best" magazines therefore, I have adopted a system that takes account of the market size as well as the payment rates.

Finally, elsewhere in this handbook are several short sections on a variety of subjects of interest to the magazine writer. These include an explanation of why some well-known magazines are not featured in the market study reports; a list of useful addresses; advice on how and where to get in touch with fellow writers of like interests; a reminder of how to submit work to editors (which should be well known, but is the sort of thing that editors repeatedly advise writers about); and some elementary advice on writing picture stories. And the handbook includes a short chapter explaining, as simply as possible, the advantages and problems of word processing — the latest and most revolutionary writer's tool (it could change your whole writing life-style).

The Future

Readers — writers and editors alike — are invited to write to the author, c/o Allison & Busby, with any information that will help with future updates of the market study reports (and any other items) in this handbook, in order to make future editions even more helpful.

2

The Market Studies

The pages that follow contain the real meat of this book: the detailed market-study reports of those magazines considered to be the best outlets for "ordinary", usually spare-time, freelance writers — those without any particular area of specialization. As has already been explained, the studies do not include specialist trade or hobby magazines nor county magazines.

The pages, which are in alphabetical order, are set out to a common format: at the top, the magazine's title plus any message included in their masthead. Beneath this, the name of the editor and the editorial address. The set of figures at the top right-hand corner are, in order from the top:

Frequency of publication   Price per issue
Payment rate £ per 1000 words*
Number of initially unsolicited non-fiction pieces used per year
Number of unsolicited short stories used per year — excluding serials

(*Often the minimum payment rate, sometimes the average. Where editors will only quote rates in my groups — see below — then the group is shown. Where the editor is unable or unwilling to cite a figure, I have made my own assessment of the likely minimum payment rate group and marked this with an asterisk (*) — thus, *Annabel* is shown as B*: my guess.)

In the case of IPC magazines whose editorial offices are in King's Reach Tower, the address is not given in full but quoted as (IPC) London SE1 9LS. In all such cases this should be expanded to read:

King's Reach Tower, Stamford Street, London SE1 9LS.

Payment rates: groups

> A = £0 – 20 per thousand words
> B = £21 – 40 per thousand words
> C = £41 – 70 per thousand words
> D = £71 +   per thousand words

AMATEUR GARDENING

W	40p
£50/1000	
NF:300	F:0

Editor: Peter Wood

IPC Magazines Ltd, Westover House,
West Quay Road, Poole, Dorset BH15 1JG

Established over a century ago, *Amateur Gardening* is a very lively
40-page weekly magazine from the IPC stable. For the freelance writer
with any detailed knowledge of gardening it offers a market well worth
investigating.

A typical issue contains about a dozen pages of advertisements.
Unsurprisingly, these are predominantly for gardening items: seeds and
bulbs, cold frames and greenhouses, fencing and shredders; but cigarettes
and film processing are also advertised. However, it is hardly necessary to
study the advertisements to determine that the readership consists of keen
amateur gardeners of both sexes and all ages. Unless you can offer solid
practical advice on some aspect of gardening, don't bother submitting
articles.

The magazine contains many "hard practical" regular columns: apart
from the editorial and news pages, there are pages of advice on starting a
first garden, advice on what to do each week and how to do it, and
answers to detailed problems. And there is a lively letters page — but no
payment is offered for published contributions.

There is also scope for the capable freelance (there is no room for
articles about the bumbling amateur). Each week there are about half a
dozen "how to" features by other than regular or staff writers; subjects
featured have included how to make a bottle garden, how to choose and
grow indoor bulbs, the origin of the name of an unusual orchid, how to
grow a particular flower, and even how to make wine from windfalls and
hedgerow fruits.

The feature articles are very detailed, always illustrated — with pictures
of the relevant plants and flowers, and of someone actually doing
whatever the articles suggests — and usually only one page long. They
vary in length, depending on the number of illustrations, from 700 words
to 1100 words. There are usually at least a couple of pictures — or there
can be half a dozen — in colour or in black-and-white, with each article.

The editor of *Amateur Gardening* gives his decisions quickly — usually
within a couple of weeks — and pays about £50 per 1000 words, plus extra
for black-and-white or colour photographs (depending on their size), soon
after publication. A good market — for gardening experts.

AMATEUR PHOTOGRAPHER
(The "AP")

```
W          60p
£50/1000
NF:150    F:0
```

Editor: Roy Green

Surrey House, 1 Throwley Way,
Sutton, Surrey SM1 4QQ

An advertisement-packed magazine, usually over 150 pages thick, devoted to the interests of the serious amateur photographer, the *AP* first appeared in 1884. Today it is only one — but perhaps "the first" — among many photographic magazines.

About two-thirds of its pages are advertisements: for cameras, lenses and other items of equipment, and for colour film processing. The average amateur photographer suffers from "gadgetitis", and the *AP* panders to this malady. It regularly tests new equipment, and in the world of cameras there is something new every week: new films, new techniques. But there are other editorial pages too.

There are a number of opportunities for the freelance writer who is also an amateur photographer. The editor says that he welcomes articles, and specifies that they should not normally exceed 750 words and should be accompanied by at least 6 photographs in either black-and-white or colour. Articles must of course have a positive photographic interest; travel features, for instance, would not normally be accepted. Black-and-white pictures should be not less than 8″ × 6″, on glossy paper; colour slides can be 35 mm or larger but must not be glass-mounted.

A typical issue contains about a dozen feature articles, all illustrated. Of these, three or four may be speculative freelance submissions; the rest are commissioned from "names" in the field, or staff-written. One recent issue contained an interview with a Fleet Street photographer on how he photographed animals, a portfolio of pictures of Wales, and a feature about a day in the country. This last feature was typical of a freelance contribution to the *AP*: it was longer than the specified length but offered basic advice on how to take better countryside pictures. The illustrations — some in colour, some in black-and-white — were not by the author; they had obviously come from the editor's stock.

The *AP* pays at least £30 for black-and-white features and a minimum of £50 for a colour feature. The payment rates are a minimum of £50 per 1000 words of text, and £8 per b/w picture and £12 for colour.

Submissions are acknowledged within two to three weeks; tentative acceptance or outright rejection can take a couple of months, publication of tentatively accepted material may be years later. Payment is made automatically in the month following publication. The *Amateur Photographer* is a good market, for the right material, and a prestigious one for writers who are also photographers.

ANIMAL WAYS
For the Younger Generation

Q   30p
£15/1000
NF:25   F:12

Editor: Elizabeth Winson

RSPCA, Causeway, Horsham,
West Sussex RH12 1HG

Animal Ways is the magazine of the younger (under-11-year-old) Junior Members of the Royal Society for the Prevention of Cruelty to Animals. (Junior Members aged 12-17 have their own RSPCA magazine called *Animal World*.)

Animal Ways is a glossy, well-illustrated 24-page tabloid magazine with a coloured cover page, a coloured two-page centre spread, and two or three of the text pages illustrated in colour. All other pages have one or more black-and-white pictures. There are no advertisements in the magazine other than for RSPCA activities and publications.

About half of the space within the magazine is taken up with editorial and staff features: letters (members only, no payment offered), animal care advice, RSPCA news, puzzles, readers' drawings and a pen-friend column. The rest of the magazine is filled with short stories and feature articles.

In a typical issue there will be perhaps three short stories about animals, often involving children. The stories are about 700 to 1000 words long and, of course, written in a simple style, with a good balance of dialogue and description. One such tale told of a mother and her young son washing a pet dog who had rolled in a cow-pat — it was really more a cautionary article than a story.

Feature articles too are simple in style and vary from interesting factual accounts to true stories involving children and animals. A typical issue contains 4 or 5 feature articles. One recent article told how a family had brought a hedgehog into their home overnight; the following day they watched the hedgehog make a nest in their garden and hibernate. Like the short stories, the articles are between 700 and 1000 words long and are always illustrated; the illustrations are not usually provided by the writer — but if you can provide a picture, this would inevitably be a plus.

The editor of *Animal Ways* emphasizes that she wishes to avoid anthropomorphism — attributing human characteristics to animals — throughout the magazine. She pays around £15 for each story or article plus £5 for black-and-white photographs and £8-£10 for colour. Decisions on submitted material can take quite a while — editorially-suitable submissions are checked by RSPCA experts for accuracy before acceptance. Payment is after publication; a copy of the relevant issue is always sent to the writer.

14

ANIMAL WORLD

Editor: Elizabeth Winson

RSPCA, Causeway, Horsham,
West Sussex RH12 1HG

Q	30p
£15/1000	
NF:30	F:4

Animal World is the magazine of 12-17-year-old Junior Members of the Royal Society for the Prevention of Cruelty to Animals. (The RSPCA magazine *Animal Ways* caters for those members under 11.)

Published four times a year, *Animal World* is a glossy 32-page magazine devoted to animals, animal care, and the world of nature. (There are articles about trees and other plant-life, and "animal" clearly covers fish, birds and insects.) The front cover, a centre-fold spread, and 5 other pages within the magazine are in full colour; every other page is illustrated in black and white. The only advertisements are for RSPCA activities and publications.

The editor uses a number of regular series: these have included articles about common trees, about antarctic seals, about wildlife generally and activities of "animal people". Such features are about 1000 words each, often illustrated in colour. Regular columns in the magazine include an editorial page, a letters page (from members only and no payment is offered), a topic for concern, and an animal care advice page. There are usually 5 or 6 one-off freelance articles in each issue and often a short story. There is also a poem, but by members only.

The freelance articles are usually about one page long — 800 to 1100 words, depending on the number of pictures included — and can be either fiction (based on fact) or general-interest factual articles. These latter have included a biography of one of the founder members of the RSPCA, another about Beatrix Potter and her animal tales and sketches, and a review of the animal in heraldry.

Many articles are based on personal experience of a close animal/human relationship. Phrases such as "Flo (a horse) and I left home at 6.30 . . ." and "I lay down in the long grass and watched . . ." are not uncommon. The short story, too, frequently revolves around a child's relationship with an animal. Editorial policy is very firm, though — regarding both fiction and non-fiction articles — in rejecting anthropomorphism.

Editorial decisions on freelance submissions are followed by checks within the RSPCA for technical accuracy. A response to the writer can therefore take quite a while. The magazine pays £15 per articles plus £5 for black and white pictures and £8-£10 for colour, after publication. A copy of the relevant issue is always sent to the writer.

ANNABEL
Today's magazine for today's woman

M	55p
B*	
NF:250	F:12

Editor: D. McColl

D.C. Thomson & Co. Ltd,
185 Fleet Street, London EC4A 2HS

Annabel is an 84-page monthly from the D.C. Thomson stable, with extra-large pages. It is, perhaps, the most "liberated" of the Thomson magazines and aims itself squarely at the modern woman. Of the 84 pages, about half have colour on them — around 30% of the colour is used in the advertisements. The cover pages are of course in full colour. The advertisements are directed at the younger woman; cigarettes, aspirins, personal hygiene and cosmetic products, foodstuffs and clothing are all featured. There are no classified advertisements.

Each issue includes columns on money matters, on medical matters and on holiday travel; there are book review pages, consumer problem pages, and the almost inevitable "what the stars foretell" page; and there are regular pages on cookery, knitting, fashion and beauty. Of greater interest to the freelance writer is the letters page which pays £2 for each letter published. And there is the chance of winning a prize for the letter of the month — which is then considered for the valuable "star letter of the year" prize. Letters, which should be sent to "Your Letters", *Annabel*, 185 Fleet Street, are best if under 200 words.

But it is the use of feature articles that makes *Annabel* so attractive to the freelancer. In each issue there are 5 or 6 "personality" interviews, at least half of which could be produced by the average freelance without special contacts. Examples of these latter features include interviews with the widow of a VC; with a round-the-world sailor, who just happened to be a grandmother; and with a married couple who collect fans. These personality articles vary in length from 1000 words upwards, illustrated with about half a dozen pictures, often in colour.

As well as the interviews, each issue of *Annabel* contains a further 15 to 20 articles, categorized on the contents page as either "Special Features" or, more interestingly, "For Fun". These articles are all produced by freelance writers without specialist knowledge; they vary in length from about 500 words up to 2000 words, but are mostly around 800 words. Typical subjects have included a "child's guide" to home computers (differentiating between bits and bytes and explaining how to cope with a floppy disc); the horrors of house-hunting; the unrecognized dangers of friendship; a light-hearted look at "un-favourite" words (from "Ms" to "unisex"); and an assurance that the age of chivalry is not yet dead.

Generally, *Annabel* seems to prefer short sentences, short paragraphs and simple, not over-long words. Titles are usually "punchy"; the features themselves are usually sprinkled with anecdotes, quotes and personal experiences.

Each issue also contains a short story which may be any length from about 1800 words up to a maximum of about 3000 words. It is seldom a "simple" romance story — although romance of course is not ignored — but the story is more a straight one: "a good read". One recent story told of how a mother adjusted to the problem of accepting that her children were growing up, with their own distinct personalities.

Annabel does not disclose its payment rates for freelance material; these are always determined by agreement with the editor. (In the view of the author, however, it is likely that they will pay at least within "rate B", plus extra for pictures.) Decisions on unsolicited submissions are not quick, but do not be discouraged by this; the editorial staff is always very sympathetic to new writers. Payment is on acceptance, but publication can be many months later. The editor always provides the writer with a copy of any relevant issue.

BUSY BEES' NEWS
and PDSA NEWS

2M   40p
£5–10/1000
NF:40   F:12

Editor: R.I. Cookson

PDSA House, South Street, Dorking,
Surrey RH4 2LB

The People's Dispensary for Sick Animals — entirely dependent on public support — publishes two linked bi-monthly magazines, both now in an A5-sized format. (The *PDSA News* will cease separate publication in 1986.) Some material is at present common to both publications.

Busy Bees' News is directed at readers under 11 years of age and is issued free to members of the Busy Bees' Club. A typical issue contains — as well as news items, competitions, pictures and cartoons — a couple of short stories and a couple of articles. The stories often tell of the exploits of animals and their "mothers". In a recent issue there were two stories: one told of the exploits of Frisky, "the funny bunny", his brothers Floppy and Bobtail, and his mother, Mummy Rabbit; the other told the tale of Lenny Lamb and his mother Mrs Sheep. There were no human characters in either story, but there was plenty of dialogue. The rabbit story was 1500 words long, the lamb one was 800 words.

The articles are also written in an almost fictional style appropriate to the readership age. One recent 1250-word article told of the writer watching the activities of a mallard duck and her ducklings. One of the ducklings was attacked by a Muscovy duck: the writer told how he rescued the injured duckling, gave it first aid and then looked after it — and the rest of the family — while it recovered.

PDSA News is produced for older — adult and teenaged — readers; it contains no stories. A typical issue will carry PDSA news items, an editorial, advice from a vet, and plenty of pictures, drawings and cartoons; and sometimes a short poem too. There are also 4 or 5 freelance articles which vary in length from about 500 to 1200 words.

Articles in a recent issue of *PDSA News* included a 1200-word factual article about peacocks (". . . early Christians regarded peacock flesh as the symbol of everlasting life"); 600 words of experienced advice on how to cope with dogs on board a boat; and a 700-word observation report on the activities of a pet cat.

The editor of the two magazines often has a large stock of articles and stories awaiting publication; he remains willing to consider new material but cautions that publication will often be delayed. Despite the variations in lengths reported above, material restricted to 700 words is preferred. The editor gives decisions on submitted material as quickly as possible — but this can take quite a while. Payment is small — £3 to £7 per item (less than £10 per 1000 words) — but is made on the author's acceptance of the offered fee.

CAT WORLD
The monthly magazine for cat lovers

M	90p
A	
NF:40	F:0

Editor: Harry Treadwell
(but write to Grace McHattie, Deputy Editor)

Scan House, Southwick Street,
Southwick, Brighton, East Sussex BN4 4TE

Cat World is a magazine of around 40 pages which proclaims that it is "An Independent Publication". About a third of its pages are taken up with advertisements for everything "catty": from cat loos and cat door-flaps through to cat litter, cat flea-powder and cat charities. It is undoubtedly, as its masthead says, a magazine for cat lovers.

The editorial pages are very much in line with the reader-image identified by the advertisements. There is a regular column about cat-care, pages of reviews of new cat-care products, and plenty of news and reports about clubs for cat-owners' and cat shows. There is also a letters page, but no payment is mentioned. A typical issue will also usually contain a well-illustrated commentary on a new or unusual breed of cat: this is not a freelance opportunity, however, unless you are yourself an expert.

The main freelance opening here is in the two-page spread "Let's talk cats". The editor says, "If you have an interesting or amusing tale you'd like to share or an unusual photo of your cat, please send it to us at *Cat World*. We pay for contributions used on this page." (He doesn't say how much he pays, though.) Typical accepted contributions to this page have been about 500 to 600 words in length and in a very personal anecdotal style. The cats are treated very much as personalities in their own right: "Luki (the cat) was sitting bolt upright in his bed . . . shrieking that he was starving." And after he was fed, "He gave an almighty hiccup and went back to bed." Three or four such personal tales are used in each issue.

Cat World is also a potential market for poetry: each month there is one poem — about cats, of course — in "Poets' Corner". Fairly traditional poems of no more than 24 short lines seem to be the preferred norm.

The deputy editor is quite quick in responding to submissions and correspondence.

CHOICE
The magazine for leisure and
retirement planning

M	80p
B	
NF:50	F:0

Editor: Roy Johnstone

12 Bedford Row, London WC1R 4DU

There is no doubt about the readership of *Choice*. It is directed specifically at relatively affluent retired couples, and at those about to retire.

Choice usually has around 70 or 80 pages with a colour cover; about a
third of the pages are filled with adverts, including three or four pages of
small ads. Of the advertising pages, about one-third often deal with
financial matters — which building society to approach, which consultant
can best manage your retirement "gold brick", etc. And about a quarter
of the advertisements are for holidays and holiday homes. Few *Choice*
readers depend solely on their state pensions.

Of the almost 50 pages of text in a typical issue, more than half are
written by staff or regular writers. Columns are provided regularly by
acknowledged experts: the editor of *DIY*, the editor of *Express Money*,
the former editor of *Practical Motorist*, etc. Several other features, such as
interviews with colourful or stage personalities, appear to be commissioned. It would seem best to ask the editor before working up
interview features for speculative submission.

But there are also several opportunities in *Choice* for ordinary freelance
contributions. A regular feature is the "Last Words" column, contributed
by readers who "feel strongly about . . . an aspect of life or Government
policy . . . and want to speak out." The editor restricts such contributions
to 700 words — and pays £20 for each one used. A similar spot is the "My
favourite charity" page, limited to 1000 words, for which the editor again
pays £20 — but to the charity rather than the writer.

Apart from these two regular, contributed, columns, there are often
four or five straight feature articles, varying between 500 unillustrated
words on a holiday island, and a colour picture plus 1500 words of
interesting facts about sundials. One recent issue also contained a
delightful 900-word article about the problems faced by the wife of an
enthusiastic fisherman. This had one black-and-white picture to illustrate
it.

Choice also features a regular letters page and pays £1 for each
published and £5 for the best each month. Most letters are short — no
more than about 100 words. Indeed, throughout *Choice*, sentences and
paragraphs are always short. The 900-word article on the fishing widow
(above) contained 26 paragraphs, averaging out at only 35 words per
paragraph.

Editorial decisions on freelance submissions take about a month.
Payment is just over £20 per 1000 words and is made on publication —
which may be some months after acceptance.

CHRISTIAN HERALD
Britain's most popular Christian family paper

W	20p
£15/1000	
NF:50+	F:50

Editor: Colin Reeves
(but write "For Malcolm Hall, Deputy Editor")

59 Lyndhurst Road, Worthing,
West Sussex BN11 2DB

Published in tabloid format, *Christian Herald* contains mainly religious news and spiritual feature material; its editorial policy is "conservative evangelical Christianity" — without being argumentative or crusading. Each issue also contains one full-page general-interest article and one short story; these provide a good steady market for the freelance writer. There are also occasional openings for fillers of about 200 to 500 words length.

The full-page general-interest article can be on almost any subject — as long as it is non-religious. (And the editor is quite specific about that: an article which made passing reference to pre-Christian religions and to ancient myths was rejected on grounds of "too much religiosity".) Typical subjects have included Colman's mustard, heraldry, China (the place), seashell collecting and various historic towns. Articles must be light and enthusiastic in tone; they must be between 900 and 1000 words in length; and they must be illustrated. Three or four black-and-white photographs are necessary for each article — but 5″ × 7″ prints are large enough. The whole illustrated article, words and pictures, earns up to £20.

The editor likes short paragraphs, specifying that they contain no more than two or three sentences. He likes short sentences too. Work on an average of 16-word sentences and 60-word paragraphs.

The short story, like the article, must be non-religious, light, moral and entertaining. It must be almost exactly 1600 words in length, to fit into a single page — which will also contain an illustration. Payment for the story is less than for the articles — £14 flat.

Advertisements usually have a religious association: for example, advertisements for the Church Army, Bible Land tours, pilgrimages, missions and charities abound, as do small ads for holiday accommodation and "Christian jobs".

Editorial policy on responding to freelance submissions is to reject, usually within 3 or 4 weeks, whatever cannot be used and to send tentative acceptance slips for material they hope to use. At busy times selection can take two or three months. After that space of time, if your submission has not been rejected, it is almost certainly accepted; if by then you have not heard you could reasonably send the editor a gentle reminder. Publication is often several months after submission and acceptance. Payment is made at the end of the month of publication; at least one copy of the relevant issue is always supplied. The magazine is very good too about returning all photographs, unmarked and re-usable.

CHRISTIAN WOMAN
The Positive Alternative

M	70p
£18/1000	
NF:50	F:12

Editor: Gail Lawther

59 Lyndhurst Road,
Worthing, West Sussex BN11 2DB

Another magazine from the same stable as the long-standing *Christian Herald*, *Christian Woman* has only been on sale for a few years. It offers an alternative to the more secular women's magazines. Each issue comprises 50-plus pages including a colour cover and several colour pages inside. Just over a third of the magazine is taken up with advertisements, around a fifth with freelance material, and the balance with staff-written, commissioned or regular material.

The advertisements are predominantly religious in content: for charities, missions, and evangelical publications. There are also several pages of advertisements for holiday accommodation in Christian homes and hotels. (Much of the accommodation appears to be geared to family needs, suggesting a readership mainly in the mid-20s to early 40s.)

Within the editorial pages there are regular columns on fashion and cookery; a regular miscellany feature called "Salt and Pepper", a Letters page (no payment offered), and two Christian opinion pages. Many monthly issues also feature a debate between two writers, who put both sides of a subject of current concern. (This feature is almost certainly commissioned by the editor.)

Of greater interest to the freelancer are the 3 or 4 apparently speculative submissions. Most of these features are Christian in content and tone. There is one opening each month for personal experience anecdotes — each about 800-1000 words long ("I was putting out a fresh Christian message over the telephone each day." "With God's help perhaps I shall one day fulfil my ambition . . ."). A few of the articles are less "preachy" though: an interview with a radio journalist explaining how she maintained her faith in her day-to-day work; how to cope with bereavement; advice on DIY and on how to press flowers. (In general, the editor prefers to be offered article ideas, rather than completed unsolicited submissions; the idea "can then be worked up in the best way for the magazine".)

In each issue there is one short story which varies in length from about 2000-3000 words. The characters are often family people — teenagers, parents and grandparents, sometimes all included in one story; the plots are "straight" (neither romantic nor religious), and without a "twist" — but the editor has said that she would welcome some more lively stories.

The editor gives decisions within 6 to 8 weeks and pays around £18 per 1000 words, on publication.

COUNTRY
The Magazine of the
Country Gentlemen's Association

M	85p
£60/1000	
NF:70	F:0

Editor:

Country Gentlemen's Association,
Icknield Way West, Letchworth, Herts SG6 4AP

A magazine produced for members of the Country Gentlemen's Association (CGA), *Country* has been published since 1901. It now appears
monthly and is produced for the CGA by Peter Carrick Associates of
Hitchin — but editorial correspondence should be sent to the CGA.

A typical month's issue will contain 50-odd pages within a colour cover.
(A likely market here for a good colour photograph — and 120 size is
always more acceptable than 35 mm for this sort of use.) Internal pages —
other than special supplements — are illustrated in black-and-white only.
Some of the content is taken up with CGA news or members' offers, and
with regular columns. There are columns (not necessarily every month)
on such subjects as angling, wine, money matters, antiques, motoring,
farming, bridge, chess, gardening, travel, book reviews and the "Country
Woman" page. As well as the regulars, there are usually four or five
"specials" — one-off freelance features — in each issue.

Typical subjects for the special features have included: the history of a
famous farmer; a commentary on the writer's favourite pubs; a tour of
locations associated with King Arthur; the export potential of elver fish;
and the history of lawn mowing. Most of the special features are
illustrated with one or two black-and-white photographs. The shortest
special feature article is approximately 1000 words, the longest 2000; but
1500 seems more acceptable. In terms of style, most features seem to have
longish paragraphs (80 to 100 words) but reasonably short (average less
than 20 words) sentences.

The readership, as exemplified in both editorial and advertising content, is basically middle-class and living in the country. The editorial pages
suggest that the readers enjoy unusual travel (a tour of Bucharest, Peking,
Moscow and Leningrad was on offer in a recent issue), are interested in
chess, wine, angling and motoring, and are predominantly male. (The
letters to the editor tend to be technical and are generally male-oriented.)

The advertisements include around 10 pages of small classified ads —
many for holiday accommodation and other property offers. The display
advertisements offer concentrated fertilizer, game guns, gun slings,
smoked salmon, wine racks and five-bar gates. All — unsurprisingly —
reinforce the image of the country gentleman interested in "hunting,
shooting and fishing". And those town dwellers who aspire to that status.

The editor usually responds promptly to freelance submissions;
although they are often well-stocked, the editor will usually accept
particularly suitable material. Publication can be long-delayed but payment is good — on publication.

COUNTRY LIFE

Editor: Marcus Binney

(IPC) London SE1 9LS

W	£1
C*	
NF:40	F:0

Country Life is a lavishly illustrated up-market weekly magazine concerned with conservation, architecture, the arts, sport and matters of rural interest. Issues of the magazine vary in size from around 100 pages up to well over 200 pages. The advertisements at the front of the magazine are mostly for country houses and a price tag of £500,000 is by no means unusual. The rest of the advertisements are for other attributes of "the good life" — expensive cars, drinks, jewellery, antiques, etc. There are three or four pages of equally up-market classified ads. Many of the readers of *Country Life* are clearly very affluent indeed.

Within the 40-60 pages of editorial matter there are nearly 30 features, mostly regular contributor- or staff-written. Regular feature articles/columns include such diverse subjects as sport, art sales, music, the theatre, motoring, farming, gardening, bridge, wine, books and fashion. There is also always a leader-page essay, generally about life in the country.

The freelance opportunities amount to perhaps seven or eight articles in any one issue, all of which require some specialist knowledge — about stock breeding, land drainage, the works of Manet, etc. The freelance with specialist knowledge of the right subject could, perhaps, produce an occasional illustrated article for *Country Life* — but there has to be some original research behind it.

Typical of the freelance material used was a recent two-page feature telling the life story of King Richard III through the buildings involved: his birthplace; where he trained as a knight; where he lived when first married; and the castles he built. This article was about 1400 words long and was accompanied by five black-and-white pictures — all just of the buildings, devoid of human interest.

The literary style favoured by *Country Life* leans towards longer sentences and paragraphs; 100 words is a very common paragraph length and sentences vary around 20 words.

There is a regular opening for one short poem; a "stand-alone" scenic or wild-life photograph is also used each week. Photographs (village pumps, weathervanes, etc.) are popular in the letters page too. The letters are not paid for but the pictures are, and the payment is good.

Country Life gives quick decisions and pays on publication — at unspecified rates.

THE COUNTRYMAN
comes from the country

Q	£1
£30/1000	
NF:80	F:0

Editor: Christopher Hall

Sheep Street, Burford, Oxford OX8 4LH

The Countryman is a 240-page pocket-sized, profusely illustrated, quarterly magazine about the countryside. It is aimed at the country-lover — but editorial policy is to reject material which sentimentalizes about the country, or which is written from a party-political position, or which supports blood sports. Within those limits, any well-written and trustworthy material, dealing with all aspects of country life and progress, is welcome.

A typical issue will contain, within its 240 pages, 70-odd pages of advertisements which clearly reflect the interests of the readership: craft products, "sensible" outdoor clothing and footwear, holiday accommodation, country books, gardening-aids and appeals for charities (for "distressed gentlefolk" or the Army Benevolent Fund) — all indicative of an upper-middle-class readership, middle-aged or older, often living in the towns but preferring the country.

There are half a dozen or so regular features — including editorial comments, a nature column, a farming feature, book reviews, a "personal view" and a sort of letters page. Apart from these regulars, the magazine is filled with freelance contributions. In a typical issue there would be about 20 articles, 10 or 12 short poems and up to 6 "picture sets".

The articles vary in length from a minimum of about 500 words (some of the picture sets have few accompanying words) to a maximum of about 1500 words. The longer articles are almost always illustrated; the shorter ones usually have at least one picture, and often more. The illustrations are sometimes provided by the writer but not necessarily; the editor has a staff photographer. (He also welcomes freelance photographs.) But not all illustrations are photographs, many are black-ink line-drawings prepared by the writer. (Some maps for instance, while good, are quite clearly not professionally drawn.)

Subjects for recent articles have included: haystack fires; the Talyllyn light railway; George Orwell's country associations; how Mum started selling teas to cyclists and ramblers; and the attractions of the aubretia plant. All of these were illustrated. Past picture sets have included a dozen pictures of the coast and scenery of Galloway and 400 words and 8 pictures (plus lengthy captions) on early "crucks". These are 14th- and 15th-century timber-framed buildings where two massive beams in each gable-end support the ridge (like a tent). Poems are usually around a dozen lines long, on country subjects, and quite contemporary in style.

Payment for articles is at the editor's direction but is always at least £30 per 1000 words and often more; pictures — which must not have been published before — are paid for over and above this.

COUNTRY QUEST
The magazine for Wales and the Border

M	70p
£20/1000	
NF:150	F:0

Editor: Brian Barratt

Centenary Buildings, King Street,
Wrexham, Clwyd, Wales LL11 1PN

Country Quest is a 60-80-page publication, much like an English county magazine, but dealing with all of Wales and the border counties. Up to about half of the pages are advertisements: for tourist attractions, holiday accommodation, and a variety of other goods and services, including boarding schools, ancestor research and country clothing. The readership would appear to be predominantly middle-aged and fairly affluent (much of it overseas). The magazine is clearly well supported by its advertisers.

Country Quest carries several regular columns and features in each issue: an editorial (which is usually a comment on a current topic), several pages about antiques, a crossword and a quarterly book review page. About four pages are given over to a very lively letters page, which does not pay for contributions. There is also a regular 1000-word freelance feature about a colourful "country character". There is no fiction and no poetry.

The main opportunities for unsolicited contributions are the feature articles — a dozen or more in each issue — most of which are illustrated. These deal with such subjects as an important and picturesque town; the story of flour supplies in bygone days; a report of an ancient custom still preserved; a historic house or monument; or a commentary on a dangerous sea trip. All are of course within, or directly related to, the circulation area. Most of these features are illustrated — at the rate of about two black-and-white pictures per 1000 words — and they vary in length from about 800 to 1300 words.

The editor advises that payment for submitted material works out at about £15 per page: the average 1000-word article, with two black-and-white pictures, not provided by the writer, occupies two pages. The rate is therefore roughly £15-£20 per 1000 words and the payment for black-and-white pictures about £7 each. Decisions are quickly given; publication is often several months later and payment is on acceptance.

DO IT YOURSELF
The home and garden
improvement magazine

M	80p
£65/1000	
NF:10	F:0

Editor: John McGowan

Link House, Dingwall Avenue,
Croydon CR9 2TA

Do It Yourself is devoted to the serious home-and-garden handyman. Each issue — which can contain anything from 70 to 90 pages — carries detailed information on how to undertake tasks about the house.

The 70-odd pages of a typical issue would contain around 25 pages of advertisements — of which some 80% are for tools and materials (the rest of the advertisements cover books, magazines, and even cigarettes for the frustrated worker). Within the features pages, too, there are items about new pieces of equipment and new products. Regular features include book reviews, answers to readers' problems and a letters page. This latter offers £5 for each letter used, plus a further £2 for illustrations — and the opportunity to win a "star letter" prize (usually a piece of DIY equipment worth around £20).

Apart from the regular features outlined above, a typical issue would probably contain three or four staff-written features and 7 or 8 freelance features — mostly commissioned. These can be anything from about 750 words to 2000 words in length — and are heavily illustrated. Two typical subjects for such features have been detailed instruction on how to make a set of shelves to fix to the back of a door; and how to renew electrical sockets safely. The "shelves" feature was accompanied by 5 coloured and 5 black-and-white photographs and a detailed line-drawing. The text was about 750 words and the whole feature made a two-page spread.

Advice in the pages of *Do It Yourself* is always specific and basic: "Clamp the two side pieces together so all ends are flush, then mark out and drill all the 9mm holes . . ."; "Using a tenon saw, cut . . ."; even: "Wipe off all excess adhesive . . . and leave . . . to set hard." Sentences tend to be rather long but words are always as simple as possible. Paragraphs average about 60 words long.

Before submitting an article, prospective contributors should contact the editor with a synopsis including, where applicable, the number of photographs or transparencies that will be supplied or needed. It is not essential that illustrations be supplied by the writer but clearly the magazine will be happier if they are. Finished drawings, however, are positively not wanted; supply rough line-drawings only for the staff artist to work from. The rate of payment for features depends a lot on the provision of illustrations etc., but the editor says that "in general it works out about £60-70 a thousand words". A "style sheet" is available on request.

FAMILY CIRCLE
The world's best-selling women's magazine

M   42p
£80/1000
NF:40   F:12

Editor: Jill Churchill

Elm House, Elm Street,
London WC1X 0BP

A lavishly illustrated women's monthly magazine, often of over 150 pages, *Family Circle* is sold at supermarket check-outs. The magazine is directed at the mother of school-age children, the 35-year-old housewife who is not short of the odd penny; but it is also read by her teenage daughter.

A recent issue contained over 70 pages of advertisements, half of which were for food. Cooking and household equipment advertisements filled a further 10 pages. The emphasis on food is also evident in the editorial pages, 15 of which contain recipes and associated pictures. Overall, one-third of the whole magazine is devoted to food. In contrast, only about 6% of the contents are about clothes.

There are regular columns on astrology, home freezing, medical news, one-parent families, style "for the larger person", new cookery products, an "agony" page, and readers' letters. (Published letters are short, 100 words maximum, and earn £5 each. Envelopes should be marked "Reader to Reader".)

A typical issue will also include a personality feature — slimming exercises with one star, how to make up your face with another, or bring up your kids like yet a third. There is also an occasional feature series telling how someone has overcome adversity. There are always features on cooking, clothes to make or buy, and on home-making — "interior-decorating-plus". These features are probably commissioned.

For the ordinary freelance writer there are only a few opportunities — but these are well-paying ones, if you can achieve them (£80 per 1000 words). Because of the "depth" required for such articles, seek editorial interest in a feature idea before starting work.

Typical freelance contributions include: how a good row can often improve a marriage; how to burglar-proof a house; and how a man too can be a "housewife". Such features are seldom less than about 2500 words long and can be as much as 10,000 words — in two parts. (But the very long features are usually book extracts, and therefore a "closed" market.)

Generally, the magazine favours an easy writing-style — short sentences and short paragraphs. Wherever possible there are anecdotes and quotes incorporated into the feature articles. Check lists too are popular, frequently used in "boxed" sections of the feature.

Each issue includes one story — or half a "two-parter". Stories or episodes are 5000-7000 words long; they are romances written for family reading and are often about people in their 30s. *Family Circle* does not use any poetry or "fillers". Decisions on submitted work can take over a month a-coming.

THE FIELD
The Country Weekly

W	90p
C*	
NF:150	F:0

Editor: Simon Courtauld

Carmelite House, Carmelite Street,
London EC4Y 0JA

The Field is a glossy weekly magazine devoted to country matters — about half of the magazine's pages will contain colour illustrations or advertisements. A typical issue is likely to have around 100 pages, about half of which will be for large country houses and town flats; a similar number of pages will offer cars suitable for the affluent country-dweller; and there will be several pages of advertisements for antiques, exotic holidays, expensive watches and alcohol. From the advertisements and the editorial content generally, the readership is readily identified as being interested in "hunting, shooting and fishing" generally, and horses in particular — and decidedly affluent.

There are regular columns on a wide variety of matters of interest to the country person, including: property, antique sales and motoring; fashion, fishing and food; farming, gardening, and the country scene generally; books, music, chess and bridge; and even a series of ducal portraits. There is also an "Answers to Correspondents" page, giving advice on pruning apple trees, and on the life-cycle of a salmon.

There is a lively (unpaid) letters page; but the photographs that accompany the letters are paid for. Recent photographs have included an unusual road sign (pointing opposite directions to the same place), a three-legged house (!) and a country scene carved on a church pew. Any writer who was competent with a camera could have provided these pictures.

There are usually 6 or 7 feature articles in each issue; at least half of these could be — even if they are not — provided by a spare-time freelance writer. In one recent issue there were illustrated features on the Lippizaner horses, the "Habitat" Conran's garden, and ski slopes around the world. The Lippizaner article was about 2000 words long with 8 colour pictures (none of which were provided by the writer), and told of a recent holiday — a package available to anyone — which included several hours of riding on the famous horses. The Conran garden article was 900 words long, again with professional pictures; the ski-slope article was also illustrated and was 1300 words long. Any good freelance could have written any of these pieces; the prudent one would have sought an editorial go-ahead first. *The Field* uses no poetry and no fiction.

FREELANCE WRITING
& Photography

Q	£1.25
£10/1000	
NF:50	F:0

Editor: Arthur Waite

5/9 Bexley Square, Manchester M3 6DB

The oldest-established of the several small British writing magazines, *Freelance Writing* is published quarterly. It consists of around 28 pages of articles, editorial matter and a few advertisements, all specifically about the writing business. It is full of good sound advice for experienced writers and beginners alike.

The articles deal with all aspects of the writing business — fiction and non-fiction, writing and marketing, at home and abroad. The majority of the articles fill two-page spreads — about 1000 words — but there are also one-pagers (450 words), short fillers of 250 words, and the occasional 1500-word feature. The editor understandably prefers articles that fit the three whole-page limits — 450, 1000, and 1500 words — and will edit down those that are just over these lengths.

Typical subjects covered in recent articles have included advice on writing books for American publishers; how to write for the religious magazines; a review of how various writers give their work "style"; and suggestions on how to make your holiday pay for itself — by writing about it. Fillers have included comments about the magazine's contents, the supposedly over-large entry fees charged for some writing competitions, and the horrific experiences of writers in dealings with vanity publishers.

The majority of the advertisements in *Freelance Writing* are for the publisher's own services. The magazine is just one of the facilities offered by Freelance Press Services: they also publish a monthly market-study news-sheet called *Contributor's Bulletin* and sell writing books (mostly American but some British), their own correspondence courses and subscriptions to the American writing magazines. And they have recently started running one-day seminars on writing, in the Manchester area. There are a page or two of classified ads — for other small writing magazines, for typing services, for criticism, and for correspondence courses and weekend writing schools. The readers of *Freelance Writing* are . . . freelance writers, at all stages in their development.

The editor is very quick to give decisions on unsolicited submissions — often only a few days — and payment, though only £10 per 1000 words, is usually made on acceptance. A helpful magazine — an important part of the British writing scene — and one that we should all support.

THE GEOGRAPHICAL MAGAZINE

M	95p
£40/1000	
NF:50	F:0

Editor: Iain Bain

1 Kensington Gore, London SW7 2AR

The Geographical Magazine is a well-illustrated monthly of around 60 pages, concerned with world geography in its widest interpretation. It looks at the flora and fauna, the nature of the terrain, and the habits of the people of countries far and wide. It also looks, with a kindly eye, at the exploits of the early explorers.

In a typical issue there will be 18-20 pages of advertisements — for travel-clothing and equipment, unusual holidays, and books about travel. There will also be advertisements for cigarettes, for whisky, and for quality cars. Readers prefer to "explore" in comfort these days.

The Geographical Magazine carries regular columns on a variety of subjects: education, politics, planning, and book reviews — plus what is effectively a gossip column in all but name, and an editorial column. More importantly from a freelance writer's viewpoint, there are several feature articles that could be contributed by a knowledgeable freelance. (The magazine identifies all writers' backgrounds — many are university lecturers but some are "just" freelance writers.)

In one recent issue there were three features contributed specifically by freelances — and a couple more that could easily have been so. The identified freelance contributions were one "straight" article, about an explorer born 150 years ago, and two pieces of photojournalism — words and colour pictures provided by a writer who had been somewhere unusual.

The 150-year-old explorer piece was 1100 words long and was illustrated with two black-and-white "archive" pictures — any competent freelance could have done the research and written it. The two photojournalism pieces were 600 words and 5 colour pictures on cloth weaving in Indonesia, and 1600 words with 5 colour pictures and one black-and-white, of mountain-climbing in New Guinea. A bit exotic, but within the capabilities of any traveller.

Other features were a 1000-word, one-colour-picture, staff-written piece about Mont St Michel, and 2000 words by an American academic about another early explorer. Given a bit of research, a freelance could have written either of these pieces.

It is wise to seek the editor's go-ahead before going too far with expensive research or travel — but he is always open to ideas for feature articles. He pays at least £40 per 1000 words, plus extra for illustrations, on publication. Decisions come quickly.

GIRL
First for fiction . . . fashion . . . pop!

W	26p
B*	
NF:0	F:30

Editor:

(IPC) London SE1 9LS

Girl is a 32-page weekly picture-story magazine from the IPC stable. A typical issue contains no more than a couple of pages of advertisements, and one of these is likely to be associated with the magazine itself. The readership — as suggested by the single advertisement, the story content, the letters page and the advice column — is in the about-to-leave-school teenager bracket.

A typical issue would contain instalments of five serials — three being photo-stories and the other two being drawn by staff artists. It is unusual for a one-off photo-story to be used, but the serials vary from the short, four-instalment stories, to longer ones of perhaps a dozen instalments. As well as the photo- and picture-stories there are always a couple of pages of very teenage fashion (bright and breezy), three or four full-page colour pictures of pop music personalities or groups, a couple of pages of pop music news and gossip, a letters page — including the inevitable "stars" column and a quiz or two — and an advice page. Letters earn £4 if you can write at that age level — they tend to be slightly heavy humour.

The editor is always willing to consider ideas or scripts for the photo- and picture-story serials: typical instalments include 25 to 35 frames and tell of the exploits of young teenagers experiencing their first associations with boys (not quite a first romance, but almost), often including Mum in the cast of characters. The adventures are all very moral, very much in the "still at school" mould.

The editor gives quick decisions on unsolicited submissions of photo- and picture-story scripts, or better, on ideas and a synopsis for these. Payment is generally good.

GIRL (about Town)

Editor: Maggi Taylor

Girl about Town Magazine Ltd,
141-143 Drury Lane, London WC2B 5TS

W	Free
B*	
NF:30	F:0

Founded in 1973, the oldest of the London weekly working-girl giveaway magazines, *Girl* is a slickly-produced magazine usually of 60 or so pages. Inevitably, about 80% of the content is taken up with advertisements, but there are always about a dozen pages of good reading matter.

Each week there is a regular one-page column of the thoughts and experiences of a modern young working man (naturally, since this is a working girls' magazine). There is also a regular one-page gossip-column — devoted to show-biz stars and others in the news. Another regular feature, "Buzz", comprises an assortment of short items: films, theatre or pop concert reviews, personality stories, news of (lunchtime-opening) exhibitions, and descriptions of new products (quasi adverts). "Buzz" is a contributed feature but an unlikely speculative market for the spare-time freelance: you would need to make arrangements in advance to avoid duplicating regular contributors' work; and you would need to be very much aware of the London "scene".

There is a regular horoscope column; there is often a page devoted to a special readers' offer or competition; and there is usually a travel feature. All of these columns and pages appear to be regular — but not formally staff — contributions; and therefore are not a market for the ordinary speculative freelance writer.

There is, however, quite often a further one-page feature — which seems to be open to the speculative freelance. A typical subject recently was advice on starting in a new job: be punctual, ask questions, don't gossip, and initially be unobtrusive rather than a pushy whiz-kid. This article was the sort of thing that any competent freelance could produce; it was about 900 words long, full of good advice, well-written and easy to read (short sentences, short paragraphs, no long words). It was illustrated with jokey drawings, probably by a staff artist.

There is no problem in determining the readership that the magazine is aimed at — the advertisements tell you loud and clear. The average reader is a girl, probably single, working in London usually as a secretary, word processor operator or typist, earning around £7000 per year, plus "perks". She is interested in both slimming and food, fashionable clothes, beauty care, foreign holidays, the latest films — and young men; but not necessarily in that order.

Editorial decisions on speculative submissions are speedy — two to three weeks usually. Payment is good, soon after publication.

GOOD HOUSEKEEPING

M   85p
£100/1000
NF:100   F:12

Editor-in-Chief: Charlotte Lessing
(but send submissions to
departmental editors:
Features: Gillian Fairchild
Fiction: Shirley Heron
Family Matters: Edwina Corner)

National Magazine House,
72 Broadwick Street, London W1V 2BP

Good Housekeeping is a blockbuster of a magazine. A recent issue had 320 pages — "and all for under a pound, you know" — but this was not typical. More than 50% of the contents are advertisements — which is how the cover price is kept so low.

Over 40% of the advertisement pages are devoted to housekeeping items such as furniture, bedding, cookers, crockery and kitchen utensils. A further 20% are for food and drinks. And there are often 30 or 40 pages of fashions, cosmetics and perfumes. (There were 5 whole pages of slimming aids in the 320-page issue: readers may be devoted to the good life, but they are as figure-conscious as the next person.) The reader of *Good Housekeeping* is likely to be in the age range 25-45 (but there are older and younger readers too), is as likely to work outside of the home as not and is fairly affluent (Marks & Spencer and Jaeger shoppers rather than avid devotees of the mail-order catalogues and BHS).

The editorial pages of the magazine are dominated by its "departmental" features, most of which are written by staff or "regulars". Many aspects of housekeeping are dealt with in regular columns — house maintenance, money, wine, travel, etc. — and there are whole departments dealing with fashion, furnishing and food. There are also something akin to "magazines within the magazine": one such, of interest to the freelance writer is called "Family Matters", taking up perhaps a dozen pages within the overall content.

Each issue will contain a short story — anything from about 2500 to 6000 words long — which is unlikely to be "romantic", other than incidentally. Basically, the short story is just (!) a very high-quality "good read".

There will also be three or four major, one-off, feature articles in each issue, but these are usually either staff-written, commissioned, or extracts from forthcoming books. There is some limited opportunity here for the freelance — if you can get an interview with, say, a literary, stage or serious music personality — but check first with the editor to find out whether she would be interested. (That way a competent and experienced freelance can often attract a firm commission.)

Of greater interest to the more ordinary freelance, the magazine often carries 1500-word articles about personal experiences and feelings, and humorous "filler" features. And in the "Family Matters" pages there are several single-page freelance articles: on subjects as diverse as heroin addiction in the family; women's clubs and associations, and what they have to offer; and how best to travel with young children. Such articles are all in the 900- to 2000-word range.

Good Housekeeping also includes a letters page — and pays £5 for each letter used. The contributions to this page tend, more than in most other magazines, to be a discussion of topics featured in recent issues; the letters are rather longer than in other magazines — often 250 words and more.

The editor(s) are fairly quick in giving decisions on unsolicited submissions. As with other National Magazine publications, payment is good, around £100 per 1000 words for non-fiction and upwards from £150 for each short story. Payment is made soon after acceptance, which is accompanied by a contract specifying the rights purchased; publication is often many months later.

THE GUARDIAN

Editor: Peter Preston

D	23p
£90/1000	
NF:400	F:0

119 Farringdon Road,
London EC1R 3ER

Unlike most of the major daily newspapers, *The Guardian* is a good —
albeit tough — market for freelance writers. It uses a lot of freelance
articles, particularly on the Travel Guardian and Grassroots pages on
Saturdays and on the Women's Guardian pages on other days. And these
are articles by "ordinary" people, by "ordinary" writers. Articles by
freelances are also occasionally used on other pages, but these opportunities are more one-off.

Articles on all pages have a common feature: they are full of solid facts
and figures, and many are about unusual, or in some way particularly
interesting, people. Even the travel articles — about interesting places of
course — bring in snippets of information about unusual people. A study
of the features published in *The Guardian* is as good as any instruction
book on how to write for publication.

Typical subjects that have appeared in various pages of *The Guardian*
include a witty but factual commentary on the writer's experiences with
cows; how to try out the delights of hot-air ballooning, for a weekend;
arranging a cycling holiday in China; and the thoughts about present-day
life of a man who had done dozens of different manual jobs, but now lived
"on the road". The travel articles need not be about exotic places,
although many are; one interesting article recently described the attractions of a weekend in Bath. All of the travel articles include details of
several ways to get to wherever the article is about, and what it will cost,
at different standards. The Women's Guardian page frequently includes
an interview with a feminine "achiever" — often a writer, but business-
women, politicians and academics have all had their day.

The articles range from a minimum of about 800-900 words up to an
unusual maximum of around 2500 words; around 1200 words looks to be
the preferred length. The writing style is better than "tabloid" but still
kept simple. The readership of *The Guardian* can best be described as
"*Guardian* readers" — a term understood by everyone: largely middle-
class, socially aware, intelligent and perhaps a little to the left of the
political centre.

The editor usually makes decisions on speculative freelance articles
very quickly — in days rather than weeks. If you can provide what he
wants, the pay is at top Fleet Street rates: not less than £90 per 1000
words.

HERITAGE
The British Review

Q   £1.40
£30/1000
NF:80   F:0

Editor: Peter Shephard

Hanover Magazines Ltd,
80 Highgate Road, London NW5 1PB

Heritage is an up-market illustrated quarterly appearing in May, September, November and February. "It is as about things worth seeing, preserving and remembering; people in their everyday lives as well as achievers and their achievements — observed in a spirit of affection." Major features in a typical issue describe attractive towns, counties, gardens and historic buildings; all are lavishly illustrated.

A typical major feature article would be 2000 to 3000 words in length, spread across 6 or more pages; and it would have at least half a dozen photos, mostly in colour. One such feature, on the legendary landscapes of King Arthur, included 12 pictures, four of which were in colour. Full-page colour pictures are commonplace, some spread on to a second page.

As well as the more major features, there are plenty of one- and two-page articles, with mainly black-and-white illustrations. Such shorter articles range from 700 words with one picture up to 1100 words and half a dozen pictures, or 2000 words and only one illustration.

Typical subjects for the shorter articles are antique street furniture, unusual buildings, and personalities of yesterday and today. One two-page 1000-word article took the reader back to the Sussex home of Winnie the Pooh, with a "Pooh map" and historic pictures. There is scope too for shorter articles; the editor welcomes 500-word illustrated "fillers" to use in a miscellany feature — and pays well for these.

The magazine's literary style is directed at the educated reader. Many sentences are about 30 words long and while paragraphs generally are an average of 80 words long, some stretch on to about 200 words. (Short sentences and paragraphs are out — particularly in the more major features.)

A typical issue contains 96 pages; advertisements are few. What advertisements there are, emphasize the affluent, traditional nature of the readership: trace your ancestry, visit Warwick castle or Bosworth battlefield, buy a picture book of Wales or a chart showing all the kings and queens of England.

Decisions on short unsolicited submissions are usually made within a few weeks; before preparing a longer feature it is clearly prudent to consult the editor. Payment at around £30 per 1000 words, plus £10 for each black-and-white and £20 for colour pictures, is made fairly soon after publication. It is helpful — and wise — to send them an invoice, which need not show the actual payment due, if not known.

HOME & COUNTRY
Journal of the National Federation
of Women's Institutes

M	32p
£60/1000	
NF:40	F:0

Editor: Penny Kitchen

39 Eccleston Street, London SW1W 9NT

An illustrated magazine of about 50-70 pages — with a colour cover and up to 10 internal colour pages — *Home & Country* is the official journal of the National Federation of Women's Institutes. Published monthly by, and circulated on subscription through the WIs themselves, it is directed at WI members and their families. The advertisements and the editorial matter reflect this (mainly rural) readership.

About a third of the magazine's pages are advertisements — for craft materials, furniture (a recliner chair, for instance), creative and other holidays, charity appeals, and places to visit. All are appropriate to middle-class middle-aged women wishing to fill their time usefully.

The editorial pages carry 7 or 8 pages of WI news and interviews plus several regular columns and features, including: cookery; health; patterns for knitting, sewing or crocheting; a gardening column (by a "name"); a financial column; a feature on pets; and an interview with a leading WI member.

There are varying opportunities for freelance contributions. For WI features, preference is almost always given to contributions for WI members; but there are several other openings for non-members.

The regular "Personally Speaking" spot is open to anyone. Past writers have included Baroness Platt, Mary Stott, and Alan Mattingly of the Ramblers Association. This "opinion" feature — which has covered such subjects as cruelty in farming, the need for owners to control their dogs, and society's attitudes to illegitimacy — is usually about 700 words long. There are also opportunities for the freelance writer to provide general women's interest articles: recent features have included advice on public speaking, on how to keep warm and on how to start a small business — each about 1000 words long. It is prudent to check with the editor before submitting such features "on spec".

For the one- or two-page Country Almanack, the editor wants shorter articles, no more than 450 words. The Almanack, which is a miscellany section, has in the past included short pieces on ploughing contests, making paper from hedgerow leaves, the Cider Museum, etc. It also includes reports on conservation projects and campaigns.

The editor acknowledges speculative submissions swiftly — but decisions can take 6 to 8 weeks. Payment is around £60 per 1000 words and pro rata for the shorter pieces, and it is usually made before publication — which can be many months later.

IDEAL HOME

M	80p
£75+/1000	
NF:30	F:0

Editor: Terence Whelan

(IPC) London SE1 9LS

Ideal Home is another of the IPC "Women's Quality Monthly" block-buster magazines with 250-300 pages each month. And it lives up well to its "quality" soubriquet; it is "perfect" bound (i.e. like a paperback with glued spine), most of the pages are in colour and it is full of articles and photographs of expensive homes and gardens.

The 264 pages of one recent issue included 157 pages of advertisements for a wide range of home equipment — bedding, kitchens, bathrooms, and lots of furniture, both trendy and traditional. The readership is undoubtedly affluent, fashionably house-proud and often slightly "way-out" trendy; neither predominantly male nor female, it is broadly in the 20-45-year-old age group.

The editorial pages of the magazine cater well to the readership: there are lavishly illustrated features about lovely homes, and about furnishing them; pictures of flowers and of gardens and their "fixtures and fittings"; advice on home-maintenance and on cooking; and there are reader offers — for microwave ovens and cases of wine. There is very little scope for the non-specialist unsolicited freelance offering since most features are either commissioned or staff-written.

Most issues, however, contain one or two short articles which could be provided by a competent freelance. In one recent issue there were short, under 1000-word, articles about credit-cards and about dealing with bureaucrats, that could readily have been written by a freelance. But such articles must be accurately directed at the up-market readership; and it would be wise to ask the editor before submitting. If an article is accepted, however, the payment is good: at least £75 per 1000 words, on publication. No fiction at all is used.

Ideal Home also contains a letters page, paying £10 for each one published. These tend to relate to recent articles in the magazine and most are about 150 words long. Write to "Letters to the Editor", *Ideal Home*, King's Reach Tower.

ILLUSTRATED LONDON NEWS

Editor: James Bishop

Elm House, 10-16 Elm Street,
London WC1X 0BP

M	£1.30
£80+/1000	
NF:20	F:0*

*But some fiction used in the special Christmas issue.

The *Illustrated London News* has been published since 1842, bringing readers the news in pictures since long before the days of *Picture Post*, *Life* or *Paris Match*. Today, it is a very up-market glossy monthly with around 120 pages, many in colour.

A typical issue will contain about 45% advertisements: more than a quarter of these — perhaps a dozen pages — will be for spirits (malt whisky, mature brandy, etc.); another dozen pages are taken up with advertisements for expensive personal accoutrements — pens, watches and the like. The rest of the advertisements are for expensive hotels, travel facilities, furniture, clothes, etc. The target readership is in the "Rolls Royce/Savoy Hotel" bracket.

The magazine has many regular columns: property, people in the news, jewellery, collecting, money, astronomy (not astrology), motoring, books, bridge and chess, among others. Other regular features are: the "Window on the World", half a dozen pages of the very best black-and-white news pictures; "For the Record", a one page, day-by-day résumé of the past month's news; and "Briefing", a dozen or so pages of what's on in the following month.

Each issue has perhaps 7 or 8 main feature articles which are always well illustrated, with the photographer's name often given equal billing alongside the author's. Many of the features are either commissioned or staff written, but there seem to be some openings for top freelance writers. Recent features have included a 2500-word profile of Paul McCartney, a descriptive piece of the same length about the trendy new face of Covent Garden, a 700-word one-page feature on Toynbee Hall, and a 900-word description of the National Trust gardens at Sheffield Park. Each of these articles was lavishly illustrated, mostly in colour; but the pictures were either specially taken by a named photographer or came from agencies. A good spare-time freelance writer — given the knowledge, or the ability to reach the personalities — could have written any of these features. A prudent one would ask the editor for a go-ahead before starting work.

Although the special Christmas issue* of *Illustrated London News* carries some fiction, this is not a market for the ordinary freelance; most of the stories are specially commissioned.

The editor gives quick decisions on non-fiction ideas and on unsolicited submissions. He pays well (£80 and more per 1000 words), normally on publication — but if this means a particularly long delay, he will pay on acceptance.

JACKIE

W	22p
A*	
NF:50	F:150

Editor:

D.C. Thomson & Co. Ltd,
185 Fleet Street, London EC4A 2HS

Jackie is a weekly colour magazine, of about 30-40 pages, for teenage girls. In a typical issue there would be 8 or 9 pages of advertisements (mainly cosmetic products and mail-order catalogues) directed at girls in the 12-16 age bracket.

The pages are filled with gossip about, interviews with, and pictures of, pop stars and groups; fashion and beauty-care advice; and advice on how to get and keep a boyfriend. The readers are much involved with their first boyfriends and worried about the possibly embarrassing situations that can arise. There is, of course, a page of advice from a couple of "older sisters" on the problems that loom large in teenagers' lives. There is also a letters page that offers £2 for each letter published and £5 or a prize for the "star letter". If you can write like a teenager — but not unless — write to Sam at *Jackie*, 185 Fleet Street.

Jackie's major interest for the freelance writer is its fiction. Each issue contains a 3-4000 word instalment of a gripping serial, the star of which is almost always a teenage girl; a short story of 2000 to 3500 words (one or two pages) which might be a schoolgirl romance, or a not-too-extreme fantasy story; and a teenage girl's first-person "true story" of about 1800 words. (If you are contemplating writing this sort of "confession", it is essential to get the words just right — today's teenagers don't use yesterday's phrases.)

As well as the conventional fiction, there are usually a couple of photo-stories — one serial and one complete story. The complete story will consist of about 27 frames covering three pages. One recent photo-story was about a boy and a girl who volunteered to help some old people, got it all wrong, but found romance themselves.

Most of the non-fiction in *Jackie* appears to be staff-written but there could be openings if you can supply the right material. In a recent issue there was a two-part feature on what to do on holiday; any competent freelance could have done this. The editor also uses features on emotional or humorous subjects; aim at about 1500 words and keep the sentences and paragraphs short.

Editorial decisions can take more than a month — but payment is made on acceptance.

JUST SEVENTEEN

Editorial Director: David Hepworth

52-55 Carnaby Street,
London W1V 1PF

2W	45p
B*	
NF:10	F:40

Just Seventeen is an up-to-the-minute magazine for fashion-conscious teenagers, published every two weeks by the EMAP Group. It is immensely "alive" and full of pictures. There are pictures of pop stars, pictures of ordinary teenagers on the streets, and pictures of fashionably-dressed teenage girls.

About a third of the 60-plus pages are taken up with advertisements and at least half a dozen of these are whole-page ads for pop records. Another 7 or 8 pages are for cosmetics and shampoos; only one or two pages feature teenage clothes (including jeans). The banks too are in evidence, seeking to persuade teenage readers to open up accounts — hopefully for life. A very definitely teenage-girl readership — and these are no shy retiring violets.

The editorial pages of the magazine are lively and stimulating. (A recent feature showed pictures of girls wearing boys' and girls' underwear — and pictures of fully-dressed boys, bragging that they wore none.) There are many pages of short illustrated items: pop news and gossip, "notice-board" items, "what's on" reports, and covert advertisements. There are usually a couple of pop star interviews in each issue and a centre-fold picture of a male pop star. There is also an advice column and a lively letters page. (No payment, except for the star letter which attracts £10.)

Each issue usually contains one or two short stories which range from 1000-2000 words in length. The stories are almost always about a teenage girl and usually about the problems of finding a boyfriend. One recent story told of a girl trying desperately to make friends with a boy — any boy — at a party; another told how a girl got talking to a boy over a disputed bar of chocolate.

Many of the feature articles — including the "star" interviews — in *Just Seventeen* are staff-written; several more are obviously commissioned. But some of these latter could easily have been offered by a freelance — for example a recent 800-word feature asking "Are you the marrying kind?" Other features have included serious treatments of the plight of 16-year-old mothers, and on how to deal with crushes on male teachers. Any writer sympathetic to teenagers' emotional problems could have offered these to the editor. It would be best to ask if the editor would be interested in an idea first though, before submitting a finished manuscript.

LATE NEWS: *Just Seventeen* is now published weekly.

THE LADY
A Weekly Newspaper

W	40p
£34/1000	
NF:600	F:0

Editor: Mrs Joan L. Grahame

39-40 Bedford Street,
London WC2E 9ER

A typical issue of *The Lady* will contain 64 pages plus the cover, divided almost equally between advertisements and editorial matter. The advertisements will include about 25 pages of classified advertisements: for holidays and holiday accommodation; houses and flats to let — at home and abroad; domestic situations vacant and wanted, and "educational". Display advertisements tend to be for items of interest to affluent, fortyish and older, women; they will also include charities, public service situations and nanny agencies.

The Lady uses no fiction but each issue will contain up to about a dozen general-interest articles contributed by freelance writers. There are also about a dozen regular columns — not open to freelance contribution — on theatre, fashion, books, pet care, gardening, etc. And there is a staff-written column of "Views and News". The leading article, "Viewpoint", is an essay of 800 to 1200 words (but 800 preferred) giving a freelance writer's controversial views on almost any subject; typical subjects have included divorce, French grammar, guardianship and thrift.

About half of the freelance articles are illustrated, usually with photographs. (The editor reminds contributors that photographs must be **taken** in black-and-white: neither colour prints nor black-and-white prints from colour negatives are acceptable.) Occasionally too, articles are illustrated with line-drawings or black-and-white reproductions of paintings. An oft-recurring article is an up-to-date exploration of an attractive town, usually in Britain; this will almost always include some anecdotal history. These articles usually spread over two pages, contain 1350 to 1500 words, and include four or five scenic photographs.

Travel articles too are frequently featured. Usually, but not always, illustrated, these can be about Europe, the Hindu Kush, China or South America; the whole world is *The Lady*'s oyster. Most of the travel articles are slightly personalized — containing details of what "I" or "we" did, and always full of facts, helpful to those following in the writer's footsteps. Lengths vary; around 1450 to 1500 words unillustrated or 1350 to 1500 illustrated are preferred but shorter pieces are also considered.

Each issue will also contain three or four unillustrated "personal experience" articles of about 800 to 1500 words. Subjects have included: how to cope with prying visitors; the perils of owning a garden swimming-pool; making a pet of a hen; and a eulogy for a pet cat. Poems too are occasionally used in *The Lady*; they seldom exceed 12 lines in length and are "conventional" rather than "modern".

The Lady can take as long as three months to give decisions on some unsolicited submissions — but "obvious" rejections often come back in a month. Payment is at the end of the month of publication — which can be several months after acceptance. A copy of the issue in which work appears is always provided and photographs are always returned. Payment is £34 per 1000 words used, plus £8 to £11 per picture used.

LIVING
Your magazine for today

M	42p
£80/1000	
NF:40	F:0

Editor: Dena Vane

Elm House, Elm Street,
London WC1X 0BP

Sold at supermarket check-out counters as an impulse buy, *Living* is a monthly magazine of over a hundred pages. Profusely illustrated — there is hardly a page without a picture — in both colour and black-and-white, it is directed at the young, fairly liberated, housewife. Features range from the problems of parenthood, through "make-up mistakes" and up-to-date fashion, to advice on coping with a major crisis or improving one's sex-life.

Overall, within the magazine's 100-plus pages there are usually over 50 pages of advertisements — about half for foodstuffs and kitchen equipment and about a quarter for cosmetics, hygiene and slimming-products. There are also occasional advertisements for products for pre-school children — picture books, rattles, etc. The advertisements all help to identify the typical reader as a 25- to 35-year-old housewife with children, holding firmly on to her youth and her liberated interests.

The editorial space devoted to fashion and food also suggests the same typical readership. The fashions featured are always up-to-date and practical rather than extreme. The lavishly-illustrated recipes range from the simple basics to the adventurous exotic.

Living is not a large market for the ordinary spare-time freelance writer. There are several regular columns, covering money matters, bringing up young children, keeping fit, health and medical problems, book reviews, and of course, the usual astrology column. These columns are not open to freelance writers. The magazine also has several staff writers who are identified in the masthead information.

In each issue, though, there are a few — three or four perhaps — identifiable openings for good solid features on subjects of real everyday importance to the readers. Typical subjects have included: coping with aged parents; living with infertility; getting the best out of the NHS; and "hard" advice on how to train your memory. *Living* uses no fiction and no poetry.

It would be wise to seek the editor's interest before working up and submitting major feature articles. It is not worth the effort of producing such features without prior editorial interest. The features are well-researched and backed up with quotes, anecdotes, check lists, useful addresses, etc. Feature articles can be up to 3000 words in length; sentences tend to be short, paragraphs often run on to 100 words. The standards of style, interest, and content are very high: payment too is high — at least £80 per 1000 words.

LONDON CALLING
The Magazine with a heart

Editor: Daphne Ayles

19 Chelsham Road,
London SW4 6NR

Q   50p
£2/1000
NF:35   F:0*

*Short story competition
run every two or three
years

The journal of the London Rechabites, *London Calling* is a "friendly" illustrated 16-page magazine. It is obviously of a Christian bent, but not stridently so, and much of its contents are of general interest. The front cover carries a photograph and the contents listing; the back cover is usually an advertisement for some organization with links with the London Rechabites.

A typical issue would contain 8 or 9 freelance-contributed articles and three or four short poems. The remainder of the magazine is occupied by news items, a "what's on" page and a variety of competitions and quizzes.

The general-interest articles cover a wide range of subjects: from memories of London sales to how to make decorative egg-cup cosies from egg boxes; from a history of the churchman "Woodbine Willie" (once of St Martins-in-the-Fields, Trafalgar Square, London) to tales of the frustrations of air travel. Article lengths vary from around 350 words (one column) to about 1000 words (a page and a half); the editor says that the shorter the article the better its chances of acceptance. She prefers contributors to write to her with a query about an article idea — and will even reimburse postage on queries.

Poems are generally about 12-15 lines in length: the editor's policy on poetry appears to be carefully adventurous — not all of the poems rhyme, nor are they all of a traditional nature (although most are).

The editor pays a token £1 for each accepted article, poem or inside-page photograph — to cover out-of-pocket expenses. At least it is payment; at least it is a friendly market; and it is all in a worthy cause. The editor has a considerable stock of accepted material though, so there is a long time-lag between acceptance and publication.

An additional item of interest to freelance writers is the annual writing competition. Sometimes a poetry competition, sometimes a short-story contest — but always something; and the prizes are currently £10, £5 and £3. Details are in the magazine, usually in the summer issue, with entries plus a small fee, due in about 3 months later. The editor is always happy to send a copy of the current issue for two first-class stamps.

LONDON'S ALTERNATIVE MAGAZINE (LAM)

W	Free
£50/1000	
NF:200	F:0

Editor: Tim Grimwade

21-25 Goldhawk Road,
London W12 8QQ

Another of London's free magazines, *London's Alternative Magazine* began life in 1977, as *London's Australasian Magazine*. It is now however much more geared to the interests of Londoners themselves and of all visitors to Britain. The magazine is not, like most of the other free publications, handed out at railway stations or pushed through letter-boxes, but is picked up from street dispensers throughout central London.

A typical issue contains about 84 pages, half of which will be normal advertisements. Roughly 15 more pages will be filled with a whole range of "what's on" listings — film, theatre, art, sport, music, books and "things to do".

The advertisements — which pay for the free circulation — are for short- and long-distance travel (European trips alongside cheap travel to Asia and Australia); for all kinds of temporary jobs — from chamber-maids to bus-drivers and computer operators to physiotherapists — in London; for cars and bicycles for hire; and for sightseeing holidays in Britain and the rest of Europe. Clearly the readership is made up of both visitors to Britain and Londoners seeking advice on leisure activities.

There are more editorial pages in *LAM* than in many of the other freebies. There are regular columns on body care, drinking and food, plus the many pages of listings referred to above. (There are also half a dozen or so pages of news and sport, in "Australasian Update" — but these pages are shrinking as the magazine's image changes.) And there are several one-off features, many of which could be supplied by any ordinary freelance. Typical of these are general articles about things to do in England and Europe. (There are freelance travel articles about far-flung places such as Penang, Australia and North Yemen too — but these require specialist experience.)

One article in a recent issue of the magazine that could have been provided by any freelance was 1000 words on holidaying in a narrow-boat on England's canals. Another fact-packed feature dealt with the places of interest that could be reached in a day's outing from London — and then expanded to look at facilities for staying overnight. There was also an illustrated 1000-word article about Christmas in Scotland. And if you can make contact with up-and-coming stars in the entertainment world, there is a ready market for short interview features.

The editor gives decisions quickly on unsolicited submissions and pays not less than £50 per 1000 words, immediately after publication.

LOOK NOW

M	65p
B*	
NF:20	F:12

Editor: Adele-Marie Cherreson
(Features Editor: Lisa Aylett)

27 Newman Street,
London W1P 3PE

Look Now is a bright monthly magazine "created and produced by" the Carlton Publishing Group — which is within the overall IPC organization. A typical issue might contain around 90-100 pages including the cover — made up of about one-third advertisements and two-thirds editorial content.

The magazine is directed specifically at the single girl aged around 20 (say 17 to 23), and either living, or dreaming of, a supposedly sophisticated life in the city. More than half of the advertisements are for shampoos, deodorants, personal-hygiene products or mail-order fashions — all fairly middle-of-the-road.

The editorial pages portray the same reader-image: a dozen pages of fashion pictures, 8 pages of beauty-care advice, advice on leaving home and coping with anorexia, interviews with pop stars and about 18 pages of information snippets, shopping advice and "what's on" listings. There is also a horoscope column, "Starscope" — currently linked with an advertising feature for the appropriate makeup for each star sign.

A typical issue would also probably contain a few feature articles, either commissioned or freelance, and a short story. There is a regular serial but this does not appear to be a market for the ordinary freelance.

One recent feature article was on how to cope with two boys at one time — or how to be one of a boy's two girls. This "Double Trouble" feature was 2000 words long and filled a two-page spread. It would be wise to check with the editor before trying to submit such a feature — most other articles appear to be staff-written or commissioned.

The short story too is usually about 2000-3000 words long. It is likely to be a romance between two youngsters — in their early 20s — centring perhaps on a first meeting, or a reconciliation. These short stories seldom have "twist" endings.

Look Now also has a letters page; it does not pay for letters but offers a prize worth over £10 for the best letter of the month.

The editor responds quite quickly to submissions and queries about possible features. Payment rates are not advised.

LOVING — with Hers

W	28p
£18/1000	
NF:0	F:400

Editor: Ms Gerry Fallon
(Fiction: Lorna Read)

(IPC) London SE1 9LS

The only remaining first-person real life — i.e. "confession" — story magazine in the IPC stable, the weekly *Loving* has absorbed the monthly *Hers*. Each issue is made up of 30-odd pages, only 3 or 4 of which are advertisements: *Loving* "lives" on its sale price. (The advertisements are for shopping catalogues, or for personal-hygiene products.) Each issue is chock-a-block-full of stories.

A typical issue will contain 8 stories, varying in length from "short-shorts" of 1000 words, up to the longest at 4000 words. There is an absolute editorial limit on the length of the stories at 4000 words. Exceed this at the risk of almost certain rejection!

All of the stories are first-person narratives. The narrator can be a girl or a boy, but is most often a girl in her late teens or very early 20s. The style of writing is colloquial — and absolutely correct for the narrator's age — without being slangy; sensual, without being explicit or erotic; and always entertaining, offering the reader a moment of escape from humdrum everyday life.

Regular features — apart from the stories — include a colour picture of a pop group, a shopping guide, a gossip column about the lives of pop stars and the inevitable astrology column. (*Loving* however does not accept unsolicited non-fiction features — so don't waste anyone's time trying.) There is also a very uninhibited advice page. In a magazine called *Loving*, it is perhaps understandable that this should deal mainly with sex-related problems: "Is our sex safe?" (using the sheath), "Is it illegal to sleep with my cousin?" and "I'm worried that I may be a lesbian!"

Loving features a regular letters page too, called "All Your Loving" — but this is really only open to regular, teenaged, readers. It is not a market for the freelance letter-writer. Writers will however find the letters a particularly useful guide to current fashions in the use of words by older teenagers and young 20-year-olds.

The editor advises a very thorough market study of *Loving* before trying to write for it — she says that many submissions indicate a lack of such prior study. She also reminds writers that the parents of readers were themselves perhaps a part of the "Swinging Sixties"; neither mums nor grannies are necessarily grey-haired old ladies sitting in their rocking-chairs a-knitting. All unsolicited stories are carefully read but the editor warns that this can take a couple of months. If accepted, though, she pays a minimum of £18 per 1000 words for the longer stories and this is on a rising scale. A minimum of £30 is paid for the short-short stories.

MiDWEEK
The intelligent guide to London Living

W   Free
£50/1000
NF:50   F:0

Editor: Bill Williamson

6-7 Cambridge Gate,
London NW1 4JR

From the publishers of *Ms London* (see below), *Midweek* is another free
weekly magazine handed out at main London rail and underground
termini. Its free distribution is, of course, paid for by the advertisements
within the magazine. Overall, the 40-page magazine contains around 26
pages of advertisements to 14 pages of editorial matter. The advertisements are mainly for jobs, but also for "kissagrams" and the like, holidays
and houses for commuters.

Unlike *Ms London*, the jobs on offer in *Midweek* are not only for
women and the editorial content reflects this mixed readership. Regular
features and columns include a "Computer Briefing" (what's new in the
world of home computers), a motoring column and a two-page spread on
"Ethnic London". The lead column is by a "personality" doing little more
than philosophizing on — his or her — life. And there is a 4-page guide to
what's on — films, theatre, books, dance, exhibitions, TV, night-life and
music.

A typical issue is also likely to contain one or two probably commissioned features and one or two apparently speculative freelance
contributions. The commissioned features could be — as in one issue —
about London's gossip columnists, or about an entertainment world
personality; 1200 words and half a dozen pictures is about average — the
pictures probably coming from an agency. The writing style throughout
Midweek is lively; the content of the features is much like that of those in
the mass-circulation tabloid dailies.

A typical subject for the shorter feature articles, which appear to be
speculatively submitted freelance work, would be an Oxford Street
eccentric. Such an article would be about 700 gently mocking words long,
based on an interview, and containing plenty of quotes and anecdotes.
(For this sort of interview, though, you don't have to make an appoint-
ment four weeks in advance, and anyone can have a go.) It is, of course,
essential that the personality is a London one — *Midweek* readers are not
much interested in out-of-town eccentrics. An accompanying picture too
might help to sell such a piece, but this is not essential.

The editor makes decisions on speculative submissions quickly — in no
more than about two or three weeks — and pays, on publication, at not
less than £50 per 1000 words. *Midweek* carries no fiction.

MOTHER

Editor: Marina Thaine

Commonwealth House,
1-19 New Oxford Street, London WC1A 1NG

M	70p
C	
NF:70	F:12

An IPC publication, although not housed in King's Reach Tower, *Mother* is a monthly magazine "bubbling over with features, ideas and things for mothers to do" — as its front cover says. Of its hundred and more pages about half are advertisements; these are for everything connected with babies and small children, and with pregnant, nursing and play-school mothers. The readership is clearly female, aged say 20 to 35, with or expecting babies and/or pre-school children.

The magazine has several regular features: there is a column by a "reversed role" father (a writer) who stays at home and looks after three children; a regular feature about family life (a different family each month); advice columns, and an astrology page for both mums and babies.

Of particular interest to the freelance writer-parent are, in each issue, a personal-experience story about the moment of birth (written by either mother or father), and another personal-experience feature called "Good Days and Bad Days". Both these regular features are in the 800-1000-word bracket, and could be written by any freelance — with the relevant experience. (A recent "good/bad" feature was written in a fictional style — lots of dialogue.) More such features are wanted by the editor.

Another interesting semi-regular feature, headed "Do You Agree?", tells how someone has coped with a problem in an unusual or contentious way. One recent piece was 700 words on how to get the kids to sleep.

These are usually three or four more 1000- 1500-word articles that could be freelance-written. One such article suggested ways to use the spare time when the kids first go off to school. Another was about school meals — this may have been commissioned, but could have been written by any good freelance.

Mother uses one short story in every issue. A recent story told of the feelings of a mother, and of the couple who were about to adopt her baby. This was beautifully told in about 2400 words. The editorial limit on story lengths, however, is "about 3000 words".

Letters are welcomed and £5 is paid for each one published; and there is a star prize — worth about £15 to £20 — for the best each month. There is a further opening for writer-mums in the "Last Word" page: *Mother* pays £3 for snippets of wit or wisdom "out of the mouths of babes" — and again, there is a star prize.

The editor responds fairly quickly (usually within a month) with decisions on unsolicited submissions and, like other IPC magazines, pays soon after publication at — for non-professionals — a little under NUJ rates. Generally, payment falls into "rate C".

Ms LONDON
London's Greatest Jobfinder

W   Free
£50/1000
NF:30   F:0

Editor: Bill Williamson

6-7 Cambridge Gate,
London NW1 4JR

A weekly magazine (varying in size, around 60-80 pages) distributed free on the streets and at the London commuter stations, *Ms London* is directed expressly at the working girl. Its free distribution is, of course, paid for by its advertisements — which take up 80% of the pages. And around three-quarters of the advertisements are for secretarial jobs in London — currently offering £7-8000 per annum. The rest of the advertisements are clearly for the girls who fill these jobs. They offer cheap travel, last-minute holidays, beauty salons, restaurants and wine-bars, astrology services — and "kissagrams" and the like. (*Midweek*, above, is from the same stable.)

Together with the advertisements — to encourage the reader to turn the pages of the free magazine — there are about a dozen pages of editorial matter. These always include several pages of reviews and reports on current activities in town — titled "Sights and Sounds" — covering films, the theatre, concerts, people and events. There is also a regular page of hidden advertising, called "Talking shop" — reporting on interesting new products in the shops.

A popular recurring feature is a profile-cum-interview with a star of the entertainment world — but this is either staff-written or specially commissioned. It is not for the average freelance.

Apart from the regular editorial features, however, there are some occasional features that could well be provided by the freelance writer — but are probably usually commissioned. A recent issue included a 2000-word review of credit facilities and how to choose between them; a lot of work had been put into this feature but any competent freelance could have done the same. Clearly, though, anyone proposing to offer such work to the editor would be wise to enquire first. (The editor says he is always willing to hear from new writers — but particularly asks them not to phone.) Very occasionally, there is also a short, more obviously freelanced, article. This can be as little as 500 words and is often a humorous personal experience.

Editorial decisions are made swiftly — two or three weeks; publication and payment also follow quickly. Payment is at least £50 per 1000 words, but the editor prefers to think in terms of "£85 – £125 for a 1500-word . . . substantial feature, and . . . pro rata".

MY STORY

Editor: Geoff Kemp

M	65p
£14/1000	
NF:0	F:120

P.O. Box 94,
London W4 2ER

My Story is a monthly magazine of about 70 pages devoted to short stories told in the first person — what used to be known as "confessions". Other than a couple of "reader offers" there are virtually no advertisements in the magazine at all; there are, however, a page or so of editorial comments about new items in the shops: slow-cookers, pots, pans and kitchen clocks — advertisements in all but name.

The few advertisements and the like are of little help in determining the age of the typical reader — but the advice column helps. This features such comments as, "My husband left me and now I live happily with the two children, aged 7 and 9 . . .", suggesting that the typical reader is perhaps 25 to 35 years old, female and married or "ex-married", with children.

The age of the typical reader is borne out by the stories themselves. One story told of (by) a 30-year-old single parent with a teenage child, another of a divorced couple who meet again — and then part again, the storyteller finding happiness in another spouse.

The stories are all first-person narratives, by a woman of around 30 years, who is usually "experienced"; and there appears to be no editorial bar on unmarried couples going to bed together — even if they are not later to get married. The love-making descriptions are by no means explicit; they are more along the lines of "and the earth really moved", or, "I had never before experienced such divine pleasure". And there is quite a lot of unfaithfulness going on: one storyteller discovers her husband in bed with her best friend — and throws him out of the house; another's husband lands up in jail, and when she discovers this, his estranged wife decides that she still loves him. All human life is here, with few holds barred.

The stories are within the wide range from 3000 to 8000 words long — but the favoured length appears to be about 3500 to 4500 words. Every contribution is illustrated with a — posed — photograph, which is an editorial provision and no concern of the writer.

The editor pays a standard £14 per 1000 words for the "confessions" — which means a 4000-word story earns over £60, and there is a market for 120 of these per year. It is a market worth looking at.

MY WEEKLY
The magazine for women everywhere

W   20p
A
NF:300   F:130

Editor: Stewart D Brown

D.C. Thomson & Co. Ltd,
80 Kingsway East, Dundee DD4 8SL

A typical issue of *My Weekly* will contain nearly 60 pages: just under one-third of the pages will be advertisements and there will be about 40 pages of editorial matter. The advertisements are mainly for foodstuffs, cosmetics and clothes — these being mostly for the young 30-year-old, but some are for older women. The readership is best summed up as being in the range 25 to 60+ — almost everyone in fact who is "young in heart".

An issue will usually contain one part of a serial, two or three short stories, and an episode in a long-running series of "Life and the Wadhams". There will be one or two celebrity interviews, a "life-style" article — one such was about the life of a lion-tamer's wife — and two or three other freelance contributions. Regular features include cookery pages, knitting patterns, astrology and a letters page. (Letters average about 80 words long, are about "the unusual, amusing and interesting things that have happened to you recently", and are paid for at £2 each — plus a prize for the letter of the week.)

The short stories are usually a balanced selection of varying lengths, including a short one of around 1500 to 2500 words and one or two longer stories of 3000 to 5000 words. They vary from the romances of 20-year-olds, through the ageless emotional tale, to the middle-aged couple reminiscing about their younger days. The stories are mainly for the 30-year-old but are suitable reading for the whole family.

The serial can be of any length from about four 6000-word instalments upwards. The serialized stories have ranged through romantic period adventures, family sagas and thriller romances. The main requirement is a strong underlying emotional theme involving warm characters with whom the reader can identify — a "good read".

As well as the bigger feature-articles mentioned above, each issue usually contains at least one "personal experience" type of article, of about 800 to 1200 words. Subjects have included: starting cycling; overhearing snippets of conversation; and "cooking disasters". The editor has said, in relation to these articles, "We like topics that our readers can identify with," and, "They should be entertaining and have a positive slant."

There are also one or two general-interest factual articles of about 800 to 1200 words in each issue. Subjects for these are wide-ranging: they have included pins, false teeth, typewriters, redheads and word origins.

Throughout the magazine, in articles and stories alike, the sentences and paragraphs are short. Sentences average about 15 words and almost never go over 25; paragraphs almost never contain more than three sentences or 60 words and many are just single sentences.

My Weekly is also a market for short articles — "fillers" — for the "This and That" page. There are usually a couple of freelance contributions each week, each about 400-500 words long. Subjects have included Friday the thirteenth, inventions, and the present-day lack of real conversation. (Fillers should be sent to "Something to Say", *My Weekly*, 20 Cathcart Street, London NW5 3BN. Those used are paid for at £5 flat.)

Generally, *My Weekly* gives decisions on unsolicited submissions in about 4 to 6 weeks. They then, however, pay on acceptance. The editorial staff — in common with all at D.C. Thomson — are very pleasant and helpful, sometimes suggesting how a rejected submission could be made acceptable. Articles, other than fillers, are paid for at about £25 per 1000 words; short stories attract a variable sum, at the editor's discretion. Publication can be many months later.

19

M	70p
£70/1000	
NF:20	F:12

Editor: Margaret Koumi

(IPC) London SE1 9LS

A magazine of around 100 pages, directed — as the title implies — at young women in their late teens, *19* is full of fashions, features and showbiz interviews. It is also strong on ideas for future careers, beauty care, and features on people "doing their own thing".

Each issue of the magazine contains perhaps 50 pages of advertisements, most of which are for shampoos, cosmetics and hygiene products. The rest of the advertisements feature a wide variety of things, from banks to pop records and from exotic cocktails to book clubs. Everything in the magazine is geared to the interests of the clearly identifiable reader — aged 16 to 20.

Apart from the "real" advertisements, each issue will always contain around 20 pages of strikingly up-to-the-minute fashion pictures. Effectively, these too are advertisements carrying, as they do, the brand names, the stockists and the prices of the clothes. And most of the photographic models are in their late teens.

The editorial pages usually contain about 8 or 9 feature articles. These are mostly commissioned features — but there is no reason why they should be; quite a few unsolicited articles are in fact bought — but the number varies considerably from year to year. One recent feature was the history of the teenagers' fashion favourite — "Doc Martens" boots; another was an interview describing a day in the life of a stripper. The boots story was 500 words long, the stripper story was about 1200 words.

Some of the other features are also written by freelances — with the right connections, and willing to do a lot of interviews and research to get the material. These — longer — features are either "star" (i.e. pop personality) interviews, interviews with young entrepreneurs, or deal with matters of social importance, such as drug-taking or "law-breaking for a cause". There is also an opening for one short story each month — between 1000 and 3000 words in length — geared, as always, to the readership.

In all cases, for *19*, write first to the Features Editor with a specific idea and a synopsis for a non-fiction feature. It is a market that demands very close attention to the editor's needs — she knows just what she wants for her very specific readership. But it is a well-paying market: NUJ rates (£79 per 1000 words) for "qualified journalists", slightly less for "ordinary" freelances. (Fiction, too, earns slightly less.)

NURSERY WORLD
The baby and child care magazine

2W	40p
B	
NF:50	F:0

Editor: David Peck

Gloucester Mansions, Cambridge Circus,
London WC2H 8HD

Nursery World is a 32-page, two-weekly magazine with a colour cover and many black-and-white illustrations within its glossy pages. One-third of the 32 pages are taken up with advertisements — for everything connected with child care: breast pumps and nappies, young children's books and educational toys. There are also 4 pages of classified ads, mainly for both private and institutional jobs for nurses and nannies, foster-mothers and Montessori teachers. The readership includes mothers (and potential mothers) and professional "child carers" — nurses and nannies; anyone, in fact, with an interest in children from pre-conception to early primary school days.

The editorial pages include news, book reviews and shopping advice; they also carry three pages of advice on all aspects of the care of children from, say, 0 to 7 years old. The average issue of the magazine also carries half a dozen feature articles. Most of these are by child-care experts but some appear to be, or could be, written by ordinary freelance writers.

Typical of recent "specialist" features are one by a nurse on pre-conception family planning — titled "Just a Twinkle in Your Eye" — and a psychologist's view of the problems of a working mother. Such expert articles range in length from 1200 to 1700 words. If, as well as being a writer, you are qualified or particularly experienced in child care, you could certainly offer a specialist feature. Bring this point out in a note to the editor.

Of more interest to the non-specialist freelance are the few more general feature articles. One recent article dealt with how children accept adult statements absolutely literally; it was filled with examples such as, tearfully, "My Dad's leg is killing him." This article was 1200 words long and could have been written by any freelance writer. In the same issue there was another freelance contribution — 700 words on how to make your own play-dough.

Although *Nursery World* does use some short stories for the under-fives, this is not a market worth considering; the editor advises that they are offered 10 times as many such stories as they can possibly use.

The editor willingly considers unsolicited non-fiction submissions but "would welcome a duplicate copy of the manuscript" — i.e. send him two copies. Decisions are made quickly, within about two or three weeks, and payment — within the range £21 to £40 per 1000 words — is made soon after publication. (Payment for commissioned work is higher and deter-mined by negotiation.)

OH BOY!

Editor:

(IPC) London SE1 9LS

W	30p
B*	
NF:0	F:300

Oh Boy! is a weekly magazine of 30-plus pages from the IPC stable, directed at the young girl in her mid-teens, who is about to leave school, or has just left. It is full of enthusiastic news and comments about pop groups, boys in general and teenage fashion. There are virtually no advertisements at all — apart from one or two disguised as news items ("what's in the shops") and where to buy things in the fashion pages.

A typical issue will contain a couple of photo-story serials and a complete photo-story; a one-page "confession" (billed as such, in a "Casebook" series), a short story and a couple of serial instalments. Nearly all of these, except one serialized book, could be provided by a freelance writer. Apart from the fiction opportunities, there is little else here for the freelance. There are pages of news, gossip and quizzes about pop stars, advice columns — teenage girls asking how to cope with boys and with parents who don't understand — pictures of "hunky" pop singers, and a letters page ("£10 for the best, £2 for the rest"). There are also fashion and beauty-care pages and, in recent issues, a hard-hitting, uninhibited and factual series on "Sex and the Single Girl". This series of articles could be provided by a freelance but is undoubtedly commissioned.

The written stories are all short: the confession — told in the first person, of course — is about 900 words long, a recent one told how a 15-year-old girl tried, unsuccessfully, to "buy" friendship; the short story is also often told in the first person, is specifically a love story (e.g. two teenage girls competing for the attentions of one boy), and is about 1100 words long; the "non-book" serial in a recent issue was a four-part one but each part is only about 1200 words — this too is often told in the first person. (This serial told of a teenage girl's pursuit of a pop singer, her adventures as she chased him, and her eventual — safe — escape back to Mum.) The morality in the stories is all very proper.

A photo-story script writer would also find *Oh Boy!* a worthwhile market; the complete stories are about 35 pictures long, feature three or four main characters, and tell of teenage love. (A recent story told of two girls working in a Job Centre and a boy in search of a job — and a girl.)

NOTE: *Oh Boy!* has recently merged with *My Guy* (also IPC).

OUT OF TOWN

Editor: Richard Cavendish

Standard House, Epworth Street,
London EC2A 4DL

M	£1
£75/1000	
NF:70	F:0

Out of Town is an 80-page glossy magazine, lavishly illustrated, devoted to the British countryside. It does not completely ignore the more picturesque towns but its main direction is towards the stately home (if it is open to the public) and the decorative garden or landscape. In fact, 17 whole pages are devoted to "The Country on Show" — a "what's on" of open houses and castles, craft exhibitions, outdoor rallies, arts festivals and point-to-point meetings.

About a quarter of the magazine's pages are taken up by advertisements; more than half of these are for holiday hotels and other aspects of the British tourist industry. The remainder of the advertisements are for "good life" items — cigarettes, alcohol, fast cars and the like. The readership is affluent, and probably largely middle-aged.

There are about a dozen regular or staff-written columns in each issue; these cover such interests as the "garden of the month", book reviews, appraisals of country hotels and restaurants, ideas for topical outings, and short travel and conservation columns. A typical issue would also contain perhaps a couple of apparently commissioned features. (Or they may be covert publicity releases.) And there are about 6 or 7 freelance features.

The freelance features in a typical issue would deal with such subjects as competitive carriage driving, advice on landscape photography (by a "pro"), the delights of an Indian summer (in Britain — there is no overseas content), and ballooning memorabilia. The minimum length of article is about 800 words; the maximum around 2000 words. Almost all features are illustrated, most with both black-and-white and colour pictures, one or two of each — but not necessarily provided by the writer. The majority of the pictures are of landscapes, gardens, houses or street scenes; few photographs, other than the street scenes, contain any people.

The editor gives decisions fairly quickly — in about a couple of weeks. Payment is at an average of £75 per 1000 words, and is made about two months after publication.

OVER 21

Editor: Pat Roberts

M	75p
B*	
NF:40	F:12

Wellington House, 6-9 Upper St Martins Lane,
London WC2H 9EX

Over 21 is a monthly magazine of over 100 pages devoted to the interests of fashionable young women — and possibly some men too. Over 40% of its glossy pages are devoted to advertisements — mostly for cosmetics, personal-hygiene products, shampoos (7 whole pages), clothes, drinks and cigarettes. The readership suggested by the advertisements is of course female, but there are advertisements for male contraceptives too — though this doesn't necessarily mean there is a male readership. This assumption about the readership is borne out by the advice column, which includes queries about how much to pay Mum for board and lodging; how seriously a 24-year-old girl should take the love of an older married man; and how to live with a lop-sided bosom.

The magazine often contains about 20 pages of fashion pictures and about a dozen pages on beauty care. (One recent article was about how "your man" could improve his appearance, and sometimes there are several pages of men's clothes.)

There are regular features on "living style" and the inevitable astrology and gossip pages. At the front of the magazine there are always several colourful pages entitled "Overall" — what's on, where to shop, what to read, which film to see and a selection of free samples, reader offers, and new gadgets.

As well as the regulars, there are a variety of special features, three or four of which could be produced "on spec" by freelance writers. Obviously commissioned features include "star" interviews (recently, a DJ and a "Dallas" personality), the confessions of a motoring correspondent and the joys of being a single girl (by a "name").

Recently potentially freelance articles — usually around 1000 words — have included living with a man for the first time, how a man evaluates a girl on a first date, and how a girl can spot, assess, and hang on to, a "Successful Man". Any competent freelance could have written these articles — and one was by a man, so there is no need to use feminine pen-names. The editor prefers a well-targeted written (never phoned) query before any submission — and tell her where you have been published before.

Over 21 also carries one short story in each issue. And they are specifically asking for stories, so even if this is not a big market, it is clearly an eager one. The stories are about 4000 words long, are "liberated" in content — and a "good read".

PATCHES

Editor:

W	24p
A*	
NF:50	F:150

D.C. Thomson & Co. Ltd,
185 Fleet Street, London EC4A 2HS

Patches is a weekly magazine of just over 30 pages, for girls aged around 12 to 15 — young teenagers. There are many illustrations — centrefold pictures of "hunky" boys in pop groups, pictures of teenage girls looking dreamy-eyed and wearing trendy clothes, and pictures of "hunky" boys and dreamy-eyed girls making up to each other in photo-stories. There are few advertisements — perhaps 4 or 5 pages — and all are directed at the needs and problems of teenagers: jobs, health and appearance.

The magazine contains several pages of news and gossip in a feature called "Info" — mainly about pop groups and other stars of the entertainment world. There are also usually several quizzes, a very friendly advice column, a horoscope page and a letters page. *Patches* pays £2 for letters — short, and very bright and breezy, and from teenage readers only — to "Postman's Knock", *Patches*, 20 Cathcart Street, London NW5 3BN; the star letter gets a £4 prize.

There are usually three stories — and a serial — in each issue; there is also often a short article (which may be staff-written, but needn't be). Two of the short stories (and the serial) are photo-stories, each of around 30 pictures, and almost always about how a girl can attract the attention of a boy she fancies — and vice versa. The main characters are often still at school, and the stories are strictly moral. There are often no more than three or four characters pictured in them and much of the action often takes place in the open air.

The third story in a typical issue is usually a first-person "true story" — told by a teenage girl and about 1400 words in length. One recent such story told of a girl recovering from being jilted by her boy friend; she sat for hours moping in the local library before she noticed the attractive boy who was also in there. Then he asked her out for a coffee.

Any non-fiction features are light and breezy. They tend to be geared to the main interest — getting a boy friend. One recent 600-word article, entitled "What is Love?", sought to differentiate between being in love with someone, and being in love just with the idea of love. All good stuff — and any good freelance could have written it.

The editor may take several weeks to respond to unsolicited submissions but then pays on acceptance.

PEOPLE'S FRIEND
The famous story paper for women

W	20p
A	
NF:20	F:200

Editor: Douglas Neilson

D.C. Thomson & Co. Ltd,
80 Kingsway East, Dundee DD4 8SL

Over a hundred years old, the *People's Friend* is truly "the famous story paper for women". Each issue is full of short stories and serial episodes — all "good reads". There is always one episode from each of two long serials and usually three or four short stories; often there is an illustrated article; there is usually a very short children's story; and there are several "reader participation" features. There is also a page or more of recipes.

The magazine is directed at women of all ages but the advertisements — occupying about a third of the 40-odd pages — and the letters suggest that the average reader is a middle-of-the-road, "ordinary" woman, probably in her mid-30s and upwards.

The stories in the magazine usually include two long ones and one short one: the longer ones are around 2500 to 3500 words long; the short one — which is usually "straight" rather than with a "twist" ending — is 1000 to 2000 words in length. The main characters can be of any age — but tend to be 30-plus; older characters sometimes look back with nostalgia to their youth. ("He stared down into the smiling face of the girl he had never forgotten. Who would have thought that such a thin girl . . . would turn into such an elegant woman?")

The serials can be family sagas or straightforward romances — always emotion-packed and occasionally tear-jerking. They are about 50,000 to 60,000 words long, in 4500-5000-word instalments.

People's Friend welcomes happy baby stories from readers — about 500 words plus a picture if possible, for which they pay £10. (Send to "Happy Event".) They also invite 300-word "memories" sparked off by a cover picture; for these — sent to "Covers" — they pay £3 each. They pay £2 too for favourite black-and-white or colour snaps sent to "Snap Happy". (Send a s.a.e. for return of the snaps.) Letters are not paid for, but earn a caddy of tea — and the possibility of a "letter of the week" prize.

A typical article was one about favourite gardens. Illustrated with 7 colour photographs (supplied by the National Trust), this was a 1000-word personalized tour ("I always enjoy having a peek into someone else's garden") around the gardens in the pictures.

People's Friend uses some poetry, sometimes in a special one-page feature. Poems used are conventional — they always have both a rhythm and a rhyme.

Payment for stories and features is on acceptance; the editorial staff, like all at D.C. Thomson, will often encourage a likely new talent.

PRACTICAL HOUSEHOLDER
For DIY & Home improvement

M	**75p**
B*	
NF:20	**F:0**

Editor: Denis Gray

IPC Magazines Ltd, Westover House,
West Quay Road, Poole, Dorset BH15 1JG

An illustrated monthly, *Practical Householder* is the IPC answer to DIY enthusiasts' needs. It is not the best of markets for the spare-time freelance writer — but there may be some scope; see below.

A typical issue of the magazine will have more than a third of the 80 – 100 pages filled with advertisements — for everything the practical householder could want. There are advertisements for substances that cure leaks, and other substances that will stick anything to anything; there are shower-fittings for enthusiastic home-plumbers; there are whole staircases; there are replacement windows; and there are taps and tools and timber.

The advertisements are not restricted to the obvious displays; there are also often about half a dozen pages of "product information" — advertisements by any other name. And there are readers' offers and competitions for DIY equipment and materials filling another 5 pages.

There can be no doubt about the typical reader of *Practical Householder* — he is a man, of almost any age between perhaps 20 and 80 and enthusiastic about doing things for himself. (Often, but not solely, to save money.)

The enthusiastic reader will undoubtedly develop better ways of doing things though — and can pass on this advice to other readers, for money. Any writer who is also a practical person and can offer such "DIY hints and tips", should write to "Passing it On", at the above address. The editor pays £5 for each hint used and there is also a star prize — such as a valuable electric drill — each month.

There are about a dozen illustrated feature articles in each issue of *Practical Householder* — but they are usually all by the paper's two staff feature writers. Initially, this does not look encouraging to the freelance writer — but one or two of each month's features could just as well be freelance-written as staff-written.

One recent staff article that a freelance could quite easily have written, was about how to make money at DIY. It contained 2500 words in 23 short self-contained sections — each section being either a suggested service to offer or advice on how to be businesslike. (By keeping accounts, making tax and VAT returns etc. — just as we writers do.)

The editor might well be grateful for a change from producing all the material in-house; think up a particularly good — and appropriate — idea; then write and ask him if he would be interested. There is a chance, if the idea is suitable, that he will give a go-ahead, "on spec".

READER'S DIGEST
World's most read magazine

Editor-in-Chief: Michael Randolph

25 Berkeley Square,
London W1X 6AB

M	£1.00
£300+/1000	
NF:0*	F:0

*But — many opportunities, hundreds per annum, for fillers, which can earn as much as £1 per word.

The British edition of the *Reader's Digest* sells about one-and-a-half million copies per month. Other editions sell many more millions of copies — worldwide. Other than for "page-end fillers" and humorous anecdotes though, it is not really much of a market for the spare-time freelance writer. The editor says quite clearly: "Most of our material is condensed from other publications or written specially for us by our own writers." He stresses however that he is always willing to consider ideas (not finished work) from professional freelance writers for *RD*-type features — but the standards are extremely high and only a full-time freelance is likely to succeed here. But it is an excellent, if tough, market for fillers.

The editor invites contributions for two main anecdote slots, "Life's Like That" and "Humour in Uniform", offering £100 for every story accepted. For the "Life's Like that" page the editor wants true stories of personal experience showing the funny side of everyday life; "Humour in Uniform" uses similar material — about present-day service life. The editor likes these anecdotal submissions to be in the form of a letter of up to 300 words — which he can edit down to 100 or so words. The prime requirement is that the story be true — and funny. Five to 10 such anecdotes are used each month; not all come from British readers.

The editor also pays at least £15 for individual page-end fillers such as the recent Keith Waterhouse comment that not only are policemen getting younger, but that numbers are getting longer: his Penguin Book, once number 1783, is now ISBN 0140017836 and his London SW5 address is now SW5 9DE. Up to 40 short fillers are used in a typical issue.

Send filler material to "Excerpts", *RD*, as above. Such short submissions are neither acknowledged nor returned; keep a copy and skip the usual reply envelope. It is sensible to submit only one item per page, typed (of course) centrally, double-spaced, with extra-wide margins all round. And put your name and address on each sheet.

It can be a long time before the *Reader's Digest* uses accepted material — and they can take up to 6 months to make a decision to accept — but they pay (well) on acceptance. They don't notify rejections — so just defer offering identical material elsewhere for about 6 months after submitting to them.

RED LETTER
For Women who love Good Stories

W	14p
A*	
NF:0	F:150

Editor:

D.C. Thomson & Co. Ltd,
185 Fleet Street, London EC4A 2HS

Red Letter is a 32-page weekly magazine, on newsprint, devoted almost entirely to fiction. There is only about one page of advertisements in a typical issue — and what advertisements there are, are almost entirely for other D.C. Thomson publications.

Apart from the fiction content, a typical issue contains several regular columns: a couple of pages of illustrated recipes; shopping, astrology and problems pages; a crossword competition, a "quiet" corner, and even a strip cartoon about a dog, "Tiny"; and a letters page. (Write to "You're Telling Me", *Red Letter*, 20 Cathcart Street, London NW5 3BN: published letters are rewarded with a prize, or £2 — specify which.)

A typical issue will contain instalments of two long-running serials and three or four short stories. The serial instalments will be 4500 to 6000 words long, the short stories from 2500 to 4500 words long — with an apparent preference for a 3500-word length.

Characters in the short stories, and main characters in the serials, are often in their early 20s; they can be married, and having (solvable) problems with their spouses, or divorced and in need of love — or, of course, single and in the same state. The serials can be period romances, detective romances, or just straight romances. All the stories, serials and short stories alike, are strongly romantic and emotional.

A typical recent short story told the tale of two young people meeting in a reference library, looking up their ancestors — and finding that they were distantly related, which did not preclude their falling in love.

The average reader of *Red Letter* — identifiable both from the characters in the stories and from the letters and problems pages — is a woman in her 20s or 30s, possibly with a small child, and not particularly affluent.

Decisions on submitted stories are given fairly quickly and payment is made soon after acceptance.

ROMANCE
Full of Unforgettable Stories

M   65p
£14/1000
NF:0   F:120

Editor: Geoff Kemp

P.O. Box 94,
London W4 2ER

Romance is a monthly "confession" magazine published by Atlantic Publishing. Each issue is made up of around 70 pages and contains about 10 stories, an advice column, an astrological forecast and a two-page spread of recipes; there is no other non-fiction content. There are virtually no advertisements at all. There is a page or so of "what's in the shops", a trailer for the following month's issue, and a page describing the treats included in the current issue of the sister magazine, *My Story*; and that's the lot. *Romance* lives on its sales.

The 10 stories are all first-person tales, all supposedly told by girls in their late teens or early 20s and working in shops, factories or offices. The readers are clearly in this same sort of bracket — and this is borne out by the letters to the advice column. Three recent requests for advice were from teenagers — one "going steady", one aged 18 and pregnant, and the other worried about how to keep her boyfriend while insisting on remaining a virgin.

Three of the stories in a recent issue were in the 2000-3000-word range; the rest were between 4000 and 6000 words long, with 4000 words appearing to be the most popular length. The content of stories is very modern: the characters often make love, and not necessarily only with the eventual favourite; boys share flats with girls — and stay celibate; wives leave their husbands and go home to mother — and caution their sisters never to tie themselves down in marriage; and a silly young office-girl has an unsuccessful but torrid affair with a married man 20 years older than her, and comes to regret it. And always there is a slightly hidden moral to the stories — they are really very close to the classic "confession" mould. Each story is illustrated with a black-and-white picture of a boy and a girl — usually kissing, or cuddling, or near to it.

The editor is very willing to consider the right sort of stories "on spec", makes decisions quite quickly, and pays a standard £14 per 1000 words, on acceptance. A fairly low-paying market, but quite a large one.

SECRETS
The Magazine With Super Stories

W	14p
A*	
NF:0	F:250

Editor:

D.C. Thomson & Co. Ltd,
185 Fleet Street, London EC4A 2HS

Secrets is just what its sub-title proclaims — a magazine full of stories. A typical issue will contain 32 pages — printed on ordinary newspaper — including a coloured cover. There are few advertisements — less than one page — and only a few regular non-fiction columns: but there are plenty of stories.

The regular columns include a crossword puzzle, an astrology page and a page of advice on readers' problems. There is also a letters page offering a choice of prizes (worth up to £5 each) for published letters. Write letters to "Pick of the Post", *Secrets*, 20 Cathcart Street, London NW5 3BN — not to Fleet Street. Another regular feature of the magazine is a short "star" profile, "People you see on TV". The fashion and beauty page is slightly unusual: whereas the rest of the magazine suggests a middle-aged readership, the fashion page features clothes for younger people — perhaps so that Mum can buy the right presents?

The stories bear out the picture of the perhaps 40-plus-year-old readership: most stories have main characters in their 40s or older, or are family-type stories with both young and old characters. A typical issue will contain episodes of two serials, each episode being 5000 or 6000 words long; the serials can be family sagas, romantic thrillers, or just plain romances. The magazine may also contain two or three short stories in the 3000-4000-word range, a "true confession" of about 2500 words, and a short-short (a *Secrets* Mini Story) of about 1000 words.

The stories are seldom just conventional romances, indeed, they are more likely to be good, straightforward or emotional stories about middle-aged couples or ladies living on their own with pets for company. One recent short-short was about a middle-aged man seeking a hotel room for the night — unsuccessfully, until he told a young couple who had a room booked for them that the room was haunted! The "confession" story varies from the norm in that the narrator is often in her 40s.

An interesting point about *Secrets* is that stories can be openly by male writers. There is no need for a female pseudonym, nor is there any suggestion that a man cannot understand romantic feelings.

The editor gives fairly quick decisions on stories and payment is made soon after acceptance. Like all D.C. Thomson editorial staff, the editor is helpful to budding writers who show promise.

SHE

Editor: Eric Bailey
(Features: Barbara Whiter)

M	70p
C	
NF:140+	F:0

National Magazine House,
72 Broadwick Street, London W1V 2BP

One of the few women's magazines that men not only read, but admit to reading, *SHE* is an exuberant publication for the "alive" woman. Its 100-plus pages are filled with enthusiastic comment on everything from cookery to sex, from cosmetics to underwear, and from clothes to "girl talk" (about men). There are never less than 70 pages of editorial matter, the remaining pages being filled with advertisements.

The colourful advertisements in *SHE* accurately reflect — as always — the readership: more than one-third of the pages are devoted to cosmetic or personal-hygiene products and more than a quarter to foodstuffs. Cigarettes and kitchen equipment also occupy significant space (5 pages each). Almost everything is directed at the bright, broad-minded, outward-looking young-thinking — middle-class — woman in her 20s to 40s: the reader that the editor is aiming at. It is the attitude of mind that is most important — that is how the editor really sees his readers.

Of the 70 pages of editorial matter, around 50 are taken up with staff-written or regularly commissioned material. There are columns on gardening, money, wine, sex problems and the stars; there are several columns by "names"; there are 10 solid pages on clothes and 4 on beauty-care; there are double pages devoted to fashion ideas and accessories; there are lavishly illustrated pages of food and drink; and there are reader competitions and special offers.

Each issue contains one short story, or part of a longer story; this fiction content can be over 20,000 words long — half of a full-length novel. It is unlikely that unsolicited freelance fiction would now find a market.

But *SHE* welcomes freelance non-fiction material. In a typical issue there will be at least a dozen feature articles provided by freelance writers. These can be as short as 800 words or can take up a full two-page spread (2500 words and at least one picture). At these longer feature-article lengths, it is probably wisest to ask the editor for an expression of interest in an idea before working it up and submitting it. (Don't forget the s.a.e. with the enquiry.)

In one recent issue, just under half of the feature articles were basically interviews — with one personality or with several "ordinary women" — and full of quotes. But they were the sort of interview that could be arranged by any competent freelance writer; not the sort where you have to work your way through layer upon layer of press aides or public relations "fronts" to get to the star. A TV producer, a circus owner and a very successful shopkeeper were among the subjects of recent interviews — and all were women.

Recent subjects for non-interview freelance articles have included an investigation into how they put holes in Gruyère cheese; slimming exercises; DIY projects and personal experience stories. There is also a series of one-page articles about historical women — which looked like a freelance opening, but is in fact a commissioned series. Generally, paragraphs go to about 100 words long: sentences average about 18 words — but the editor assures writers that the magazine can accommodate most competent writing styles; it is the subject matter and treatment that's really important.

Smaller opportunities for selling material are the letters page (£3.50 for all used and £10 for the best — they average about 100 to 200 words in length — and £5 is paid for one jokey "Odd Snap" each month); and the "Prize Boobies" page, which pays £3.50 for each funny misprint. There is also the "I Say!" column — about 400 words putting "your point of view on any subject" — which is paid for at the usual rates, even though it doesn't always say so in the magazine.

SHE takes about two weeks to make a decision on submitted work. When a feature is accepted, a contract is sent for signing and then the feature is paid for, promptly. Publication can then be long after; SHE buys for stock. You will be sent a proof of the edited article before it is used, and asked to check it through for factual accuracy.

THIS ENGLAND
**. . . for all who love our
green and pleasant land**

Q	£1.50
£10/1000	
NF:80	F:0

and

EVERGREEN
This and That and Things Gone By

Q	£1.50
£10/1000	
NF:80	F:0

Editor: Roy Faiers

P.O. Box 52, Cheltenham, Glos. GL50 1YQ

This England is a glossy quarterly, founded in 1968, devoted to the glories of the English heritage. It is strong on nostalgia, and beautiful — traditional — things. It uses a lot of pictures, both colour and black-and-white, some as full-page spreads.

A typical issue contains several features forming part of continuing series: such subjects as popular family hymns, English county regiments, characters from the classics and a gardening series are typical. But there are opportunities for one-off freelance contributions too. A regular "Cornucopia" feature uses short fillers of around 300 words — preferably illustrated with one or two black-and-white photographs. There are opportunities too, for longer one-off features — again, preferably illustrated.

Typical freelance contributions in recent issues have included a 700-word article about the Burlington Arcade in London, a black-and-white illustrated two-page spread — 6 pictures, all of people, and approximately 1000 words — about Yorkshire craftsmen, a timely 1800-word feature about George Orwell, and a three-page, 1600-word illustrated article about a Sunday school magazine. (Jesus wants me for a "Sunbeam".)

This England uses a fair amount of poetry, both in a "readers column" of requests and as features. There can be as many as 10 "meaningful" poems — of the traditional, rhyming sort — in an issue. There is also an editorial service to provide the words of old music-hall monologues on request. The magazine does not use any new fiction.

A typical issue contains 84 pages: 5 or 6 pages of advertisements — mainly small — and the remainder filled with editorial material. There is hardly a page without an illustration, often in colour, and often occupying the full page. The advertisements are directed at the older, more affluent members of society — offering Range Rover accessories, "ancestor-tracing" and expensive rocking-chairs. The only display adverts are for the magazine's own products — e.g. a red cloth rose or a St George symbol.

This England is fairly quick in rejecting definitely unwanted MSS — three weeks recently — but can be considerably longer with marginally acceptable material. The editor says it can take three months for a decision and, "material is invariably returned without further consider-ation to an over-zealous contributor". (So don't chase him.) Payment, after publication, is at about £10 per page for black-and-white pictures or for text. (This works out at a minimum of about £10 per 1000 words. Black-and-white pictures tend to be used at about quarter-page size.) Colour pictures earn £50 for the cover or £20 per page internally.

The publishers have recently launched a new sister publication entitled *Evergreen*. This new quarterly magazine is published from the same address and shares the same editor, Roy Faiers. Its needs are much the same — with the important difference that it also welcomes material on Scotland and Wales. It is a pocket-sized magazine and thicker than *This England*, and because of the different size of the pages, it pays at £10 per 1000 words rather than per page.

The editor of *Evergreen* says that he will welcome general non-fiction material about famous and infamous British people, the beauty of Britain's towns, villages and countryside, and features about British crafts, traditions, folklore and history. The tone of the magazine, like that of *This England*, is unashamedly old-fashioned and reflective.

The lower limit on length of articles for *Evergreen* is 250 words and the upper limit is 2000. And the editor quite clearly says that illustrations, whether photographic or drawings, will improve the chances of having work accepted. He specifies that illustrations, whether black-and-white or colour (120-size much preferred) should generally be of outdoor scenes and contain (human) life in the picture.

Poetry too is welcomed. The editor asks that it be "meaningful" rather than "clever" and that not more than three poems be submitted at any one time.

All work submitted for *This England* is also automatically considered for possible use in *Evergreen* — and vice versa. You do not need to submit work twice. As for *This England*, decisions on submitted material can take as long as three months, so don't worry about the time — and don't chase the editor unless you want an instant rejection slip.

THE TOWNSWOMAN
The magazine of the
National Union of Townswomen's Guilds

M   25p
£35/1000
NF:20   F:0

Editor: Hazel Thompson

2 Cromwell Place, London SW7 2JG

The Townswoman is a monthly 48-page magazine devoted to the interests of the members of Townswomen's Guilds throughout the country. Much of the magazine is therefore, inevitably, devoted to news of national and local concern to members, and of what members are doing.

The magazine is produced and published for the Townswomen's Guilds by Litharne Ltd of Stratford-upon-Avon — from whence come the cheques in payment for accepted work. And Litharne clearly help to make the magazine pay its way by attracting advertisements to its columns. A typical 48-page issue will carry about 16 pages of advertisements: for TG "things" — diaries, recipe books, etc.; for various charities of interest to public-spirited women; for arts and crafts for readers themselves to indulge in (*Townswoman* readers are not just TV watchers — they do things themselves); and for places to visit — alone or in a group of TG members. There are half a dozen pages too, of classified advertisements — for holiday homes, activity weekends, medical self-help and travel opportunities. All are geared to a readership in its 30s and older.

In many issues there are several short — 250 to 800 words — anecdotes and reminiscences by TG members; and there are usually several feature articles, which look to be freelance-written. The magazine has very rarely used fiction in the past, but the possibility of using fiction in the future has not been ruled out.

Recent freelance feature articles have included a 1000-word profile of Marie Curie (and the editor has used short pieces on other famous women in the past); a 500-word feature, with three pictures, about renovating a historic house; and 850 words of advice on how the elderly should manage their finances. There have also recently been one or two much longer (2500-word) freelanced pieces, about which it would obviously be prudent to sound out the editor in advance. In this context, the editor has said that she would be particularly interested in considering ideas for "personality interview" features.

The editor prefers most unsolicited articles to be limited to about 650 words. That size allows an advertisement, or perhaps a picture, to be fitted into an attractive one-page layout. The editor pays about £25-£30 for her favoured 650-word articles, and pro-rata for other lengths; she is not over-quick in giving decisions on marginal pieces — but the best features may warrant immediate acceptance. Payment promptly follows publication, though, and the editor always provides a copy of the issue in which a writer's work appears.

TRUE ROMANCES
with Truly Yours

M   65p
£25/1000
NF:0   F:130

Editor: Heather Jan Brunt

12-18 Paul Street,
London EC2A 4JS

A monthly magazine of about a hundred or so pages (80-120), published by Argus Consumer Publications Ltd, *True Romances* carries fashion, beauty and cookery pages — and lots of fiction. Each issue contains an average of perhaps a dozen short stories. As with its sister magazine, *True Story*, all the stories in *True Romances* are told in the first person; but they are not in the conventional "confession" mould. They are just straightforward romantic stories — from a first-person viewpoint.

The stories vary from "short-shorts" of 1500 words up to about 5000 or 6000 words in length. The most popular length is about 2-3000 words. The characters in the stories tend to be in their early 20s — two stories in one recent issue brought in the heroine's twenty-first birthday party. And the stories are mildly "liberated" — the characters can be living together before marriage, there can even be an affair involving a married, not yet divorced, man with a single girl. One recent short-short story was a very romantic, but not sensual, description of the first evening and night of a young couple's honeymoon. Older characters — grandparents for instance — sometimes appear in the stories, but only peripherally.

The advertisements reflect a readership in its 20s and early 30s. Within the 96 pages of one recent issue, 36 were advertisements; of these, 15 were for cosmetics and personal-hygiene products. Cigarettes, baby foods and toys occupied a further seven pages and a variety of furniture, food, and fashion products took up the rest of the space. All of this is indicative of a young, slightly down-market reader, possibly with a small child, and anxious to relive — or experience vicariously — her earlier romances. The age of the typical reader is borne out in the problems page which deals generally with the sexual and romantic problems of girls in their early 20s.

The editor pays not less than £25 per 1000 words for these first-person stories; decisions are usually made within three or four weeks and payment is made on acceptance.

TRUE STORY
Escape to a World of Romance

M	65p
£25/1000	
NF:0	F:140

Editor: Dorothy Baldock

12-18 Paul Street,
London EC2A 4JS

True Story is another of the publications of Argus Consumer Publications Ltd. It is a monthly magazine, varying between 80 and 120 pages, devoted entirely to "true-to-life" stories. It is not an ordinary "confession" magazine, though. The stories are all romances and are all told in the first person, but there is none of the traditional "sin, suffer and repent" confession-story content.

True Story is well supported by advertisers: the average 40-plus pages of advertisements are predominantly for foodstuffs, cosmetics, soaps, tooth-pastes and other hygiene products. And there are a surprisingly large number of advertisements for children's clothes and toys. The readership would appear to be mainly married women in their early 30s with young children. But it is clear from the advice page that there are also some younger readers, in their 20s, with live-in boyfriends. On the whole the readers are "catalogue-shoppers" — slightly down-market.

The regular features of the magazine include a page or two of recipes, a knitting pattern, a beauty feature, a review of new things in the shops, a horoscope page and a problems page. It will probably also contain a couple of very short "interest" pieces. All are produced by the staff, though, or by regular commissioned writers. There are no freelance openings here.

Each issue contains 10 to 15 short stories, all told in the first person. The stories are very much like those in other women's magazines, and not a bit like the stories in the "confessions". They tell of romantic meetings, of the tiffs of happily married couples, of the innocent friendship of two young women, and of the relationship of a child to a step-parent. All straightforward plots treated very professionally.

The story lengths vary from "short-shorts" of 1500 words up to about 5000 or 6000 words (3000 words is a good, and popular, average length). There is also a regular serial, but this is not open to freelance submission.

The editor pays not less than £25 per 1000 words for first-person stories; decisions are usually made within three or four weeks and payment is made on acceptance.

WEEKEND
— and Titbits

W	27p
C*	
NF:200	F:50

Editor: David Hill

Northcliffe House, London EC4Y 0JA

A typical issue of *Weekend*, which absorbed the title of the IPC magazine *Titbits* when this closed down in mid-1984, contains around 40 heavily illustrated pages and a whole lot of pacy news and feature items. If the freelance writer can give the editor exactly what he wants, it is a good market — but it is a hard one to crack.

Some idea of the readership can be gleaned from the advertisements. In a typical 40-page issue there will be about 9 or 10 pages of advertisements: roughly half for cigarettes and the other half for mail-order goods or home-shopping catalogues. These suggest a slightly less affluent reader.

The age of the typical reader is, in this instance, best judged from the letters and advice pages: the emotional problems range from those of 18-year-old girls to those of middle-aged married women; the health page gives advice on "Mum's arthritis" and on "Fred's coronary"; most of the ordinary letters are from married women with smallish children — but there are almost always some from men readers too. The readership is broadly based, with ages ranging from the late teens to the early 50s, and including both men and women. A real family magazine. And any work for *Weekend* has to relate to this wide readership.

The magazine is chock-full of news items and illustrated features about people. Everything is short: the stories and features themselves, and the words, sentences and paragraphs within them. It is hard to find a four-syllable word, a sentence over 20 words or a paragraph over 40. All very easy reading.

There are a host of regular features in the magazine. Of particular interest to freelance writers — beginners and old hands alike — is the letters page. Contributions for this page are about 100 to 120 words long (in three or four paragraphs), are usually amusing and are always warmly human. All published letters receive £10; the star letter of the week gets £30. (Many a well-researched article earns less!) Write to "Mailbox", *Weekend*, Northcliffe House. A recent star letter told how a grandmother started making meals for her grandchildren during a school meals dispute — and now continues because it gives her a new interest, a new purpose.

Another small money-earning feature is the "How's That Again" feature: for this, send examples of unintentional humour in print — one recent item was a misprint from an Irish newspaper's TV programme listing, "7.20pm — News for the dead". *Weekend* asks for the error, plus the paragraphs above and below it, to be stuck on a postcard, marked with the name of the source newspaper (and your own name and address, of course) and sent to "How's That Again" at the same address as above. For all items used they pay £3.

Other regular features are a double-page spread of photographs of stars of the entertainment world — often in embarrassing situations; an Editor's chat page and a deliberately provocative column by a staff writer; a page of advice on sexual problems, and another on general health matters; pages on stars, gardening, antique collecting and motoring — and a children's page.

Of importance to freelance writers with ambitions beyond the letters page are about 4 or 5 articles per issue and a very short short story (about 700 words on average). There are more feature articles than the few that are mentioned but the remainder show signs of being bought in from America and are therefore inappropriate to the present assessment.

The three or four interesting feature articles in a typical issue vary from about 800 to 1300 words in length, illustrated (in black and white only) with pictures of the people to whom the articles relate, and are all filled with quotes and anecdotes. Each such feature article is based on one or more interviews; the subjects of the features are not necessarily famous — just interesting. One recent feature article dealt with a group of religious London cabbies working out of Heathrow; it included many interesting quotes about their beliefs.

At least one of the freelance articles is usually of more general interest — a collection of surprising facts and amusing stories about a single subject. One recent short, 600-word, article was about rearing babies; it included reports about edible nappy-pins and the advantages of keeping babies in a warm, womb-like padded box for the first year! There is also occasional scope for very short, 250-word, illustrated snippets about amusing animals or children — such items are best written around the picture, which must be a good one.

The editor usually responds fairly quickly to submissions, even tele-phoning if he is particularly interested in something. (But don't sit waiting by the phone — it may never ring for you.) Payment is good, and on acceptance; publication can be many weeks later.

THE WEEKLY NEWS
The Week's Best Buy

W	18p
A*	
NF:few	F:0

Editor: W.F. Lindsay

D.C. Thomson & Co. Ltd,
Albert Square, Dundee DD1 9QJ

The Weekly News is a 28-page tabloid-sized weekly newspaper geared very much to the Coronation Street and quiz-game viewer. Advertisements in the paper, which take up the equivalent of about 5 pages, include those for mail-order clothes and catalogues, patent medicines, life assurance, and a wide range of bargains by post. The readership is of all ages, but tending towards the older person; of both sexes, but more women than men — although there are 4 packed pages of sporting news; and down-market.

As well as the regular columns — motoring, your stars, TV, and health — there are human-interest features and profiles of show-biz personalities, but these are not much of a market for the ordinary freelance. There are also a few shorter items that are little more than a collection of stories built around a recent occurrence; these could be freelance- or staff-written. There is no fiction at all.

The Weekly News is, however, interested in receiving letters, hints and general fillers from readers — basically as reader-participation. In each issue, the reader is invited to send in "genuine and original":

"Letters" — £10 for the best, prizes for the rest;
"Top Tips" — £5 for the best, £3 for the rest;
"Marriage Lines" — £10 for the best, others £5;
"Meet the Family" — as for "Marriage Lines";
"Laugh Lines" — £2 for each joke published.

And the paper uses a lot of each of the above — each issue is packed with readers' contributions. There are also opportunities for personal love and problem stories; these however are usually the result of a reader writing to the editor — who then offers staff assistance in writing up the story, and pays £25. ("Confession" type fiction is not what is wanted.)

The letters are usually amusing — how a parrot learnt to call a visiting dog's name to the consternation of the dog — and always short (100 words average). "Top tips" have included sticking Velcro on the phone and on a pen, and how to frost the rims of drinks glasses. Tips are only 20 to 30 words long. "Marriage" and "Family" items too are amusing and short. Jokes are short, 20 or 30 words each; they are used throughout the pages as fillers.

WOMAN

W	30p
B*	
NF:100	F:50

Editor: Richard Barber

(IPC) London SE1 9LS

One of the biggest-selling of the weekly magazines published by IPC, *Woman* is made up of 60-plus colourful, heavily illustrated pages. Roughly one-third of the pages are taken up with advertisements and two-thirds with editorial material. The average reader is in her late 20s to early 40s, is married, perhaps with children; and if she is at work, may well be in a non-executive post. But the magazine is taken by a very wide readership, spreading well outside the "target" image.

Within the 20-odd pages of adverts, about 8 are likely to be for items of food. The rest of the advertisements cover a wide range of goods, including cigarettes, cosmetics, medical preparations and clothes (both underwear and "street" fashion). In common with many other women's magazines, *Woman* also often features special "reader offers" — holidays, exercise bikes, clothes, etc. All support the image of the typical reader.

The editorial pages cover a very wide range of topics: there are regular columns or features on food, clothes, beauty-care, health, consumer affairs, horoscopes (of course) and readers' problems. There is a lively letters page called "You & Us" — the editor pays £5 per letter and £10 for the best of the week — which also incorporates a regular reader-contribution, "How I Coped". (Around 600 words maximum length and always written by a woman, this would be a good freelance opening.)

Along with the regular features there are a variety of commissioned feature articles: every issue seems to include two or three "star" interviews — with both men and women in the news — and two or three "heavy" features. One issue contained an investigation into the dangers of nuclear waste on British beaches and another into incontinence.

There are usually one or two feature articles in each issue, however, that could be submitted "on spec" by a freelance writer. One such article was 700 words about ears! It showed how a person's character could be assessed by studying the shape and protuberance of their ears; it was, of course, illustrated with the ears of several well-known personalities — royalty, pop singers, film stars, etc.

Each issue of *Woman* contains a short story and a 4000-5000-word episode of a serial — by a "big name". The short story can be anything from 1500 to 3000 words long; the characters are usually in their 20s and the story is almost always romantic.

WOMAN AND HOME

M   70p
£79/1000
NF:20   F:12

Editor: Sue Dobson

(IPC) London SE1 9LS

Woman and Home is a big-format monthly magazine from the IPC stable; it usually has around 180 pages. More than half the pages are taken up with advertisements: of these, a quarter are for food (and slimming) products; a quarter are for good-quality furniture and household equipment; and another quarter are for clothing, cosmetics, etc. The typical reader seems to be a comfortably middle-class woman, probably in her 30s or older. (There are ads for children's clothes and toys, and the fashion pictures show a woman of around 30.)

Woman and Home has no advice page to help confirm the assessment of the reader, but the feature pages support it. There are regular features on home design and décor, cookery, beauty, gardening and fashion; there are stylish knitting patterns and craft features; and there are specialist courses in advanced cookery: all indications of affluent women in the 30+ age bracket, with traditional values.

Each issue of the magazine contains long (10,000 to 15,000-word) instalments of one or two major serials. These serials are "powerful" with a strong romantic element — though this is seldom the main story. One recent serial was about an American woman stranded in Nazi-occupied France and working with the Resistance movement.

Woman and Home also contains a short story of about 3500 words each month. The main character is frequently a women in her 30s, the plot tends to be romantic, or with a romantic twist; and the morals are always irreproachable.

There are many feature articles each month: most of these are commissioned or linked to the launch of a new book or a film. But there are usually a few features that could have come from ordinary freelances.

Past features have included a review of what Mum discovered from her 11-year-old daughter's schoolbook; how the Palace of Westminster was burnt down and rebuilt; and a humorous account of a search for a suitable hat. These features — which are not necessarily accompanied by pictures — are from 750 words to 2000 words long.

The regular columns cover selecting wine, safeguarding money, choosing books for the reader and for children, collecting antiques, family health, and astrology. There are also a couple of free-ranging celebrity columnists, and occasional reader competitions and promotions.

The features editor can usually give fairly quick decisions on non-fiction submissions; it can take longer for decisions on fiction. Payment at NUJ rates, currently £79 per 1000 words, is made soon after acceptance.

WOMAN'S JOURNAL

Editor-in-Chief: Laurie Purden, MBE
(Features Editor: Louis Jordaan)
(Fiction Editor: Christie Hickman)

(IPC) London SE1 9LS

M	85p
D	
NF:20	F:12

Woman's Journal is one of IPC's "Women's Quality Monthly Magazines". (Others include *Ideal Home* and *Homes and Gardens*.) It is a thick magazine — "perfect" bound, i.e. like a paperback with glued spine — often of around 200 or more pages. More than half of the pages are usually filled with "quality" advertisements: a large proportion are for cosmetics, perfume, etc., there are many pages of advertisements for clothes and shoes, and there are plenty of food, drink and cigarette advertisements. There are surprisingly few pages of household advertisements — furniture, crockery and kitchen equipment.

The editorial fashion section too often includes a dozen or more pages of pictures of "quality" clothes — including some for men. From advertisements and editorial pages alike, the average reader comes across as a lively, intelligent, often professional, woman in the 25- to 45-year age range, with modern and sophisticated interests.

Woman's Journal is not a particularly large, or easy, market for the ordinary general-interest freelance writer. A typical issue might contain 8-10 feature articles, but most will be commissioned. There are frequent profiles of interesting personalities: one recent issue contained interviews with a 40-year-old film actor, a high-spirited 30-year-old duchess, and an elderly flower painter. One or two of the other features, however, suggest that they were offered to the editor as ideas and given the go-ahead, rather than direct editorial commissions. Recent features of this type have included a "personal experience" report on a vasectomy (which could hardly have been commissioned from just anyone!) and a 2500-word commentary on how often nowadays, when public figures die, they are quickly shown to have had feet of clay.

Woman's Journal has regular columns on many subjects: collecting, gardening, films, books, music, money, travel, wine and horoscopes. And there are large sections of the magazine devoted to fashion, beauty, and food. Any ideas for one-off features need to be outside these areas.

The magazine usually carries a book extract or a short story. The short story can be anything up to 10,000 words long — one recent story told of a divorced couple who met 25 years later and contemplated starting over, but didn't. Many of the short stories are American reprints.

The features editor responds quickly to suggestions and submissions and pays on acceptance.

WOMAN'S OWN
Britain's Best Read Magazine

W	30p
B*	
NF:30	F:0

Editor: Iris Burton
(But address letters etc. to head of appropriate department)

(IPC) London SE1 9LS

Woman's Own is not a very good market for the ordinary, spare-time freelance writer. On the editorial page they say, with regret, that "we cannot accept unsolicited fiction manuscripts"; most of the non-fiction features too appear to be commissioned rather than speculative submissions. They are willing, however, to consider non-fiction — but initially, ideas only.

A typical issue will contain around 60 pages. Only about a quarter of these will be used for advertising; more than half of which will be devoted to cigarettes, foodstuffs and slimming aids. About 20 of the editorial pages will be taken up with regular features — columns and standard features such as fashion and recipes. There is a regular gossip column, an "our experts advise" column, the usual problems page, a medical advice column and a horoscope page. And there is a lively letters page paying £5 for each letter published and £10 for the "star" letter. (Write to "Letters Page".)

The advertisements and the various "reader response" pages suggest that the average reader is a woman of about 20 to 35 years old, often married, and very conscious of her figure. She is perhaps less liberated in her ideas — more conventional — than are the readers of some other women's magazines.

Several of the non-fiction features in a typical issue will be interviews with major stars of the entertainment world. In theory, there is some scope for the freelance to submit ideas for such features and gain a commission but in practice, such commissions will almost certainly be given mainly to full-time freelances. One recent issue, however, contained an illustrated feature about the benefits of the seaside: negative ions in the air, sea-water massages, exotic sea-foods and even the pleasures of eating seaweed. A competent freelance could well have won a commission for such a feature.

Woman's Own is a small and difficult market for the part-time freelance: leave it to others — unless you have a really sure-fire idea for a feature. (But *Woman's Own* is interested in knitting and other craft patterns — not really within the scope of this handbook.)

WOMAN'S REALM
Where the quality of family life matters most

W   24p
£30/1000
NF:30   F:50

Editor: Judith Hall
(Fiction: Sally Bowden)

(IPC) London SE1 9LS

Woman's Realm is not a big market for the freelance article writer — but it takes one short story and a 6000-word instalment of a serial each week. A typical issue of the magazine will consist of around 60 pages, just over a quarter of which are taken up with advertisements.

A quarter of the ads are usually for food-stuffs but books, magazines and financial services take up another four or 5 pages; all indicative of a somewhat mature reader — 30 and over. This reader identification is supported by the editorial pages: there is a children's page at the back of the magazine, directed at the reader's 7- to 14-year-old children; the letters page includes references to "my teenaged son"; and the regular columns cover such subjects as child care, pets, money and "beliefs".

The editorial content of a typical issue includes — apart from the regular columns mentioned above — half a dozen or so pages on food (well illustrated recipes building into complete menus) and as many on clothes (knitting and sewing patterns usually accompanying photographs of the fashion models).

Each issue is also likely to contain a "personality interview" feature, undoubtedly commissioned — but if you have an idea for such an interview (about 1000 words in length), contact the editor and you may get a go-ahead. Other than such interviews, there is often a single, 1000-word, "advice" article — on slimming techniques or the like; but again, prior editorial approval would be prudent.

The regular short story is usually about 3000 to 4000 words in length, the main character is often in her 30s or older, and the subject is usually about interesting personal relationships: it could be a flashback to the main character's own love affair, or the beginning of a romance for one of her children. The story is paid for, on acceptance, at about £140 and upwards. The serial is a good solid romantic story, often in a historical setting; it is usually bought as a book and cut to length by the editor.

There is a regular letters page: £3 is paid for each contribution used; there is no "star letter" prize; published letters are not more than 100 words long.

WOMAN'S STORY
— with Romantic Confessions and Tender

M	65p
£25/1000	
NF:0	F:120

Editor: Gill Pilcher

12-18 Paul Street,
London EC2A 4JS

Woman's Story is the third of the monthly short-story magazines published by Argus Consumer Publications Ltd. A typical issue contains just
under 100 pages, around 40 of which are taken up by advertisements.
About a quarter of the advertisements are for cosmetic and personal-
hygiene products, 5 pages are devoted to clothes, 5 to food and drink
products, and 5 more to children's clothes and toys. And there are
advertisements for furniture and for things like vacuum cleaners —
house-proud people's things. In all, the advertisements — and the letters
to the advice column — suggest a readership in the later 30s, and perhaps
slightly up-market compared with the other two Argus women's magazines.

There is nothing in *Woman's Story* for the non-fiction writer — but it is
a good market for the short story or "confession" writer. In each issue
there are currently 10 or 11 short stories and an instalment of a serial.
Most of the stories are in the first person — but there are some in the third
person. And because this is not a "confession" magazine, authors get
bylines — whether the stories are told in the first or the third person or
told by a man or a woman.

The characters in the stories are usually in their late 20s and 30s, and
sometimes slightly older. The plots are rather more "liberated" than some
other story magazines: one recent story told of a wife's reaction to her
husband's affair. (She was mad at him, he lost his job, they separated for a
while, and then she took him back. And, of course, he then got a better
job.) The advice column in the magazine carries several similar tales.

The short stories are mostly 3-4000 words in length but stories up to
5000 words are also accepted. There are also usually one or two shorter
stories, in the 1500-2500-word range.

The editor usually makes decisions on short stories in about 4 weeks
and pays around £75-£90 for a 3000-word story, on acceptance.

WOMAN'S WEEKLY
World's Best-Selling Women's Weekly
Magazine — famed for its cookery

W	28p
£30/1000	
NF:0	F:50

Editor: Brenda McDougall

(IPC) London SE1 9LS

One of the oldest women's magazines still on sale today, and retaining its well-known purple front cover, *Woman's Weekly* is nevertheless very much a best-seller. A typical issue of 60-plus pages will carry about 14 or 15 pages of advertisements.

The editorial pages are in the classical women's magazine mould: romance, recipes and royalty. A typical issue would contain a short story, instalments of two serials, and perhaps a book excerpt. Non-fiction is almost entirely confined to the regular features. There are columns on religion, gardening, child care, fashion, the stars, and an advice column. And there are always several pages of knitting and sewing patterns, along with recipes and reader offers — all lavishly illustrated.

The advertisements and the editorial pages all point towards a somewhat mature readership. The advice column includes references to "my son of 23 . . ." and "My days are full of household things . . . and looking after the children." And the advertised goods suggest a somewhat less than affluent readership.

The freelance market in *Woman's Weekly* is largely restricted to the three fiction opportunities — the short story and the two serials — and the serials are not for the spare-time freelance. The short story is usually 3000 to 4000 words long (but up to 5000 is acceptable), is always strongly romantic yet restrained and very moral. The main characters tend to be in their late 20s or older, and they often appear to be more sophisticated than the average reader — thereby encouraging the readers' fantasies.

The serials, the episodes of which are about 5-6000 words long, are equally as romantic as the short stories; they can be period fiction; they frequently bring in older characters to support the main protagonists — who tend to be in their late 20s. Like the short story, the serials too are a "good read".

Payment for the short story is at least £120; payment for the serials is "negotiable". Payment is made on publication. Decisions take up to 6 weeks.

WRITER
incorporating Writers' Review

Editor: Sydney Sheppard

United Writers Publications Ltd,
Ailsa, Castle Gate,
Penzance, Cornwall TR20 8BG

Q	£2.00
£5/1000	
NF:16	F:0*

*But regular short story
competition, see below.

One of the handful of small-circulation British writers' magazines, *Writer* is a well-produced publication of 60-odd pages; it is sold mainly on postal subscription. The editorial pages as such contain no fiction, but there is a rolling short-story and poetry competition in each issue. (Entry for each quarterly competition is free with a fresh-dated entry coupon from the magazine. The rolling prizes are small — £5 — and there is no other payment for publication. All "issue winners", however, are then voted upon by readers for the year's best story and poem, for which the prizes are currently £40 each.) There is also a separate "Picture-a-Poem" competition in each issue — write a poem about a given picture — for book prizes and (unpaid) publication.

Apart from the competitions, which take up nearly 30 pages in each issue, there are up to 20 pages of editorial comment, readers' letters, market information and book reviews; and 7 or 8 pages of advertisements — mostly for United Writers' books.

Freelance contributions usually include at least one analytical article about poets and poetry, and two or three articles giving advice on writing techniques. Typical articles have included suggestions on how to write romantic novels, how to get ideas for articles, how to sell features about ordinary people, and how to "hype" your own book.

Lengths vary from about 500 words up to about 1500 — with an apparent preference for the 1000-word article, which makes a nice two-page spread. The editorial office — it is a small, family operation — is often slow in responding to submissions and correspondence, but non-reply often seems to indicate acceptance. Payment comes after publication, and in keeping with most of the small "writing trade" magazines is low: £5 per 1000 words (but we owe it to beginning writers to help where we can). And the magazine is quite a "good read".

THE WRITER'S VOICE

Editor: Mrs Chriss McCallum

Asia House, 82 Princess Street,
Manchester M1 6WH

Q   £1.25
£20/1000
NF:15   F:16

A quarterly writer's magazine, *The Writer's Voice* was first published in December 1983. It is a nicely printed, pocket-sized 48-page publication, directed at all writers — but mainly at new ones. In each issue there are 4 or 5 freelance-contributed articles about the writing business; these are seldom more than 850 words long — the editor's specified limit. There are also perhaps a couple of anonymous advice-features on technical matters — how to count words, entering competitions, choosing the right words, presenting manuscripts, etc.; and there are always a few pages of in-depth market study (not unlike the study pages of this book and a source of up-dating material).

The Writer's Voice also publishes poetry and fiction. Each quarterly issue contains half a dozen or so short poems, ranging from haiku, through "pictorial layout" to modern free-form verse. There are also 4 short stories in each issue. These are "straight" stories, not often romances (but this is chance rather than policy); and the editor limits them to a maximum length of 1750 words.

Articles and short stories are paid for at a flat £15 each: poems at £5 a time. There is a writing competition of some kind in each issue. Every two or three issues this is a story contest: the theme is set by the editor, the length is clearly specified (often 1500 words maximum), and entries have to be accompanied by a form or token from the magazine. Prizes for the stories have, in the past, been £50 and £25; the winning stories are then published — and earn a standard reproduction fee of £15 in addition to the prize money!

The editor's policy is for the magazine not to carry advertisements within its pages (leaflets are sometimes enclosed in the mailing envelopes); the editor wants to use all the space for text — and at the same time hopes to preserve as non-commercial a flavour as possible. The magazine lives on its subscriptions.

The overall tone of *The Writer's Voice* is at present very slightly arts-oriented — but the editor is seeking a balance between the poetry side of writing and the needs of the hard-up hack. She tries to select material that would be "saleable in the general market rather than that which might only find a home in the trendy 'arty' magazines".

The editor responds quickly to ordinary — "non-competition" — submissions and cheerfully pays on acceptance. On the whole, a nice (if small) market to work for, and a very attractively produced magazine which circulates regularly to many publishing houses and other magazines. It is becoming a useful shop-window.

WRITING

6M	65p
£10/1000	
NF:4	F:0

Editor: Sean Dorman

4 Union Place, Fowey, Cornwall PL23 1BY

Writing is a duplicated, typewritten magazine published twice a year in what the editor refers to as a "pair of linked issues". Much of the same material appears in the second of each pair of issues; the net result, from a freelance writer's marketing viewpoint, is no better than an annual publication.

The 48 pages of the magazine contain about 10 pages of advertisements which are mainly for the magazine itself and the services — chiefly a manuscript society — of the editor. And of course, the other writing magazines advertise in *Writing* on a reciprocal basis.

Apart from the advertisements, each issue contains a chapter from one of Sean Dorman's own books, hot from the typewriter. His books mostly tell of life in rural Ireland when he was a child, or of the literary circles of London and Paris in his later years. Each issue of the magazine also contains an unusual selection of letters to the editor: these are either advertisements in all but name, for writers' services and competitions; or strange overseas enquiries about the magazine.

The freelance writer's interest in the magazine — apart from reading it — is in its use of poems and what the editor calls "homilies". Each pair of issues contains three poems and three "homilies" — which are short advice articles on the writing business. The editor specifies that poems shall be no shorter than 8 lines and no longer than 24; the homilies are limited to 300-350 words, a single page. The poems are fairly conventional; they always make sense, and sometimes rhyme. The homilies are on various subjects; recent ones have been about getting ideas for plots, writing for local newspapers, and about being an article "ideas man".

The editor is not particularly quick in deciding on which material he will use but he pays fairly soon after publication — at a fixed £3 for either poem or homily. He always supplies a complimentary copy of the issues in which a writer's work appears.

3

The "Best" Markets

Any assessment of the "best" magazine markets for freelance writers is inevitably going to be subjective. Every writer has his or her own "favourite" magazine — often the one that most readily accepts the writer's output. Certainly I have my own favourite magazines — and they are not merely the ones at the top of the list that follows.

For this book, though, I have endeavoured to apply an objective method of listing magazines in "merit" order. I have looked at those which offer markets to both non-fiction and fiction writers, and treated them even-handedly; I have sought to make allowances for the way that editors treat their freelance contributors — which may not necessarily be within editorial control (perhaps the accounts section is slow); and I have made some allowances for the magazines that welcome letters and/or poetry. I have developed a marking system and from that, an overall mark for each magazine. I do not pretend that my marking system is the only one that could be developed; I do claim to have applied it as fairly as possible. I have no brief for any one magazine over another.

Where editors have told me their payment rates per 1000 words, I have used that figure; where they have only identified a "payment group" I have used that; and where they have not been able or willing to cite any payment rate, I have made my own assessment — and marked this with an asterisk (*).

The basis of the marks for payment rates and for the number of freelance submissions — fiction or non-fiction — bought per year is shown in the table opposite.

I have given 10 marks for quick acceptance or rejection (roughly under one month) and 0 marks for slow decisions; similarly, there are 10 marks or 0 marks for payment on acceptance, or after publication. The market for general fiction and non-fiction is — in my view — of greater overall importance than that for letters or for poetry — so there are only 5 or 0 marks for these markets.

Having marked all of the above considerations, I have assessed an overall mark from the following calculation:

Overall Mark = (Pay mark × total market mark) + decision mark + "payment when" mark + letters mark + poetry mark.

Thus, for say *Christian Woman*, which pays £18 per 1000 words, buying 50 articles and 12 stories per year and taking rather a long time over decisions and paying only on publication, the marks are:

£18 = Group A = mark of 2

50 articles = mark of 4; 12 stories = mark of 2. 4 + 2 = total 6

Slow decisions, payment on publication, no letters, no poetry = 0

Overall mark is therefore (2 × 6 = 12) + 0 = 12.

MARKING BASIS

PAYMENT £/1000 wds	GROUP	MARK	NON-FICTION *or* FICTION BOUGHT P.A.	MARK
0 − 20	A	2	0 − 20	2
21 − 40	B	4	21 − 50	4
41 − 70	C	6	51 − 100	6
71 +	D	8	101 − 200	8
			201 +	10

THE BEST MARKETS

Ranking	MAGAZINE	Publishing Group	Frequency	Price	Payment/1000 wds	Payment "mark"	NF per annum	NF "mark"	Total market		Decisions "mark" 10/0	Payment "mark" 10/0	Letters "mark" 5/0	Poetry "mark" 5/0	OVERALL "MARK"
									F per annum	F "mark"					
1	Weekend	—	W	27p	C*	6	200	8	50	4	10	10	5	0	97
2	Guardian	—	D	25p	90	8	400	10	0	0	10	0	0	0	90
3	Good Housekeeping	NM	M	85p	100	8	100	6	12	2	10	10	5	0	89
4	SHE	NM	M	70p	C	6	140	8	0	0	10	10	5	5	78
5	Amat. Gardening	IPC	W	40p	50	6	300	10	0	0	10	0	0	0	70
	London's Alt. Mag.	—	W	Free	50	6	200	10	0	0	10	0	0	0	70
7	Annabel	DCT	M	55p	B*	4	250	10	12	2	0	10	5	0	63
	Mother	IPC	M	70p	C	6	70	6	12	2	10	0	5	0	63
	Out of Town	—	M	£1.00	75	8	70	6	0	0	10	0	0	5	63
10	My Weekly	DCT	W	20p	A	2	300	10	130	8	0	10	5	5	56
11	Family Circle	Elm	M	42p	80	8	40	4	12	2	0	0	5	0	53
12	True Romances	Argus	M	65p	25	4	0	0	130	8	10	10	0	0	52
	True Story	Argus	M	65p	25	4	0	0	140	8	10	10	0	0	52
	Woman & Home	IPC	M	70p	79	8	20	2	12	2	10	10	0	0	52
	Woman's Journal	IPC	M	85p	D	8	20	2	12	2	10	10	0	0	52
	Woman's Story	Argus	M	65p	25	4	0	0	120	8	10	10	0	0	52
17	Amat. Photog.	IPC	W	60p	50	6	150	8	0	0	0	0	0	0	48
	The Field	—	W	90p	C*	6	150	8	0	0	0	0	0	0	48
19	Woman's Realm	IPC	W	24p	30	4	30	4	50	4	0	10	5	0	47
20	Country	CGA	M	85p	60	6	70	6	0	0	10	0	0	0	46
21	The Lady	—	W	40p	34	4	600	10	0	0	0	0	0	5	45
	Oh Boy!	IPC	W	30p	B*	4	0	0	300	10	0	0	5	0	45
	Woman	IPC	W	30p	B*	4	100	6	50	4	0	0	5	0	45
24	Reader's Digest	RD	M	£1.00	300	8	0†	4	0	0	0	10	0	0	42
25	Country Life	IPC	W	£1.00	C*	6	40	4	0	0	10	0	0	5	39
	Heritage	Hanover	Q	£1.40	30	4	80	6	0	0	10	0	0	5	39
	Jackie	DCT	W	22p	A*	2	50	4	150	8	0	10	5	0	39
	Patches	DCT	W	24p	A*	2	50	4	150	8	0	10	5	0	39
29	Ideal Home	IPC	M	80p	75	8	30	4	0	0	0	0	5	0	37
30	Country Quest	—	M	70p	20	2	150	8	0	0	10	10	0	0	36
	My Story	Atlantic	M	65p	14	2	0	0	120	8	10	10	0	0	36
	Romance	Atlantic	M	65p	14	2	0	0	120	8	10	10	0	0	36
33	The People's Friend	DCT	W	20p	A	2	20	2	200	8	0	10	0	5	35
	Secrets	DCT	W	14p	A*	2	0	0	250	10	0	10	5	0	35
35	Midweek	—	W	Free	50	6	50	4	0	0	10	0	0	0	34
	Ms London	—	W	Free	50	6	30	4	0	0	10	0	0	0	34

THE BEST MARKETS

Ranking	MAGAZINE	Publishing Group	Frequency	Price	Payment/1000 wds	Payment "mark"	Total market NF per annum	NF "mark"	F per annum	F "mark"	Decisions "mark" 10/0	Payment "mark" 10/0	Letters "mark" 5/0	Poetry "mark" 5/0	OVERALL "MARK"
37	The Writer's Voice	—	Q	£1.25	20	2	15	2	16	2	10	10	0	5	33
38	Living	Elm	M	42p	80	8	40	4	0	0	0	0	0	0	32
39	Choice	—	M	80p	B	4	50	4	0	0	10	0	5	0	31
	Girl	IPC	W	26p	B*	4	0	0	30	4	10	0	5	0	31
	Red Letter	DCT	W	14p	A*	2	0	0	150	8	0	10	5	0	31
42	Loving	IPC	W	28p	18	2	0	0	400	10	0	10	0	0	30
43	The Countryman	—	Q	£1.00	30	4	80	6	0	0	0	0	0	5	29
	Home & Country	WI	M	32p	60	6	40	4	0	0	0	5	0	0	29
45	Freelance Writing	—	Q	£1.25	10	2	50	4	0	0	10	10	0	0	28
46	Busy Bees' News	PDSA	2M	40p	10	2	40	4	12	2	0	10	0	5	27
	Do It Yourself	Link	M	80p	65	6	10	2	0	0	10	0	5	0	27
48	Geographical	—	M	95p	40	4	50	4	0	0	10	0	0	0	26
	Girl (about Town)	—	W	Free	B*	4	30	4	0	0	10	0	0	0	26
	Ill. London News	Elm	M	£1.30	80	8	20	2	0	0	10	0	0	0	26
	Look Now	Carlton	M	65p	B*	4	20	2	12	2	10	0	0	0	26
	Nursery World	—	2W	40p	B	4	50	4	0	0	10	0	0	0	26
53	Just Seventeen	EMAP	2W	45p	B*	4	10	2	40	4	0	0	0	0	24
	19	IPC	M	70p	70	6	20	2	12	2	0	0	0	0	24
	Over 21	—	M	75p	B*	4	40	4	12	2	0	0	0	0	24
56	Cat World	—	M	90p	A	2	40	4	0	0	10	0	0	5	23
	London Calling	—	Q	50p	2	2	35	4	0	0	10	0	0	5	23
58	Woman's Own	IPC	W	30p	B*	4	30	4	0	0	0	0	5	0	21
59	Christian Herald	Herald	W	20p	15	2	50+	6	50	4	0	0	0	0	20
60	This England	—	Q	£1.50	10	2	80	6	0	0	0	0	0	5	17
	Evergreen	—	Q	£1.50	10	2	80	6	0	0	0	0	0	5	17
62	Woman's Weekly	IPC	W	28p	30	4	0	0	50	4	0	0	0	0	16
63	Pract. Householder	IPC	M	75p	B*	4	20	2	0	0	0	0	5	0	13
64	Animal Ways	RSPCA	Q	30p	15	2	25	4	12	2	0	0	0	0	12
	Animal World	RSPCA	Q	30p	15	2	30	4	4	2	0	0	0	0	12
	Christian Woman	Herald	M	70p	18	2	50	4	12	2	0	0	0	0	12
67	The Weekly News	DCT	W	18p	A*	2	few†	2	0	0	0	0	5	0	9
	Writer	—	Q	£2.00	5	2	16	2	0	0	0	0	0	5	9
	Writing	—	6M	65p	10	2	4	2	0	0	0	0	0	5	9
70	Townswoman	—	M	25p	35	4	20	2	0	0	0	0	0	0	8

† = mark adjusted for many "fillers"

4

Magazines That Are Not Good Markets for "Ordinary" Freelances

Many famous magazines are not included in the market study reports elsewhere in this handbook. This is because, for various reasons, I do not consider that they are good — i.e. worthwhile — markets for the ordinary, spare-time freelance to tackle. But some of these "non-markets", while not suitable for speculative articles or short stories, do offer opportunities for letters, fillers, and even poetry: some of these are listed below, together with others which offer little opportunity.

New Statesman 14-16 Farringdon Lane, London EC1R 3AU

The *New Statesman* (80p weekly) takes articles, generally on political and social issues from a left-of-centre viewpoint, mainly from "names". Until you are elected to Parliament, this market is probably not worth trying to write for. But the *New Statesman* welcomes short newspaper cuttings — stuck on a postcard — for their feature "This England"; such cuttings need not necessarily be funny, just very English. They pay £3 for each cutting used. The *NS* uses some poetry, which tends to be slightly political in its content but fairly traditional in its form. There are usually a couple of poems in each issue, each about 12 lines long.

New Statesman also runs a vaguely literary competition in each issue. A recent competition sought "polite remarks guaranteed to get rid of guests who look like staying for ever". One of the winning entries, each of which received £3, was, "The drink's run out." Judges are often such personalities as John Cleese or John Wells.

The Spectator 56 Doughty Street, London WC1N 2LL

The Spectator, which is 75p per week, is another "names only" market. Editorially, it is right-of-centre and its contributors often appear to be part of the London literary scene. *The Spectator* also runs a weekly literary competition which is perhaps slightly more intellectual in character than that in *New Statesman*. One recent competition required entrants to write 12 lines of blank verse — with several strict sub-conditions. Winning entries are paid £6.

New Society 30 Southampton Street, London WC2E 7HE

An IPC weekly magazine selling at 70p, *New Society* is all about the social sciences; it is virtually the trade magazine for social workers (and many jobs are advertised in it). As such, perhaps inevitably, it is somewhat left-of-centre in its editorial stance. And it is, from the freelance writer's viewpoint, not much more than just another "names only" magazine — unless you are a specialist in the social sciences. And unlike those above, it does not have a regular competition with cash prizes or a (paid) letters page.

New Scientist Commonwealth House, 1–19 New Oxford Street, London WC1A 1NG

Again, an IPC publication, appearing weekly at 90p per copy, *New Scientist* is a very prestigious news magazine for scientists. As far as possible though, it presents "heavy" scientific information in a form understandable to ordinary people. If you are of a scientific bent and can interpret the work of scientists, it may be a possible market for you as a freelance writer. Otherwise, no. It has a letters page which does not pay, and there is a weekly competition with a £10 book-token prize — but like the rest of the magazine, for very science-orientated people only.

Private Eye 6 Carlisle Street, London W1V 5LG

Over the years, *Private Eye* has almost become part of the Establishment it so successfully, and continually, lampoons. It is a magazine, appearing weekly at 40p per copy, that literally has to be seen to be believed: it is full of spoof headlines, spoof advertisements (at least, I think they are spoofs — it is hard to tell), cartoons and short essays. There also lots of newspaper "boobs", funny radio comments, pictures, etc., sent in by readers. Any alert person — with the right sense of humour — will find an occasional amusing item in his/her daily life; and *Private Eye* is in the market to buy them.

Each week, *Private Eye* reminds its readers that they will pay between £5 and £15 for cuttings, anecdotes, etc., for their various regular columns: "Pseuds Corner" (pomposity anywhere); "I Spy" (a reader's photograph, usually of an amusing, often juxtaposed, street sign); "Wimmin" (over-the-top feminism), "Colemanballs" (boobs by radio and TV announcers); and "True Stories" (hilarious but true news items). An example of the latter classification was a report that an American computer will produce unbelievably accurate forecasts of the weather for the next five days — but takes ten days to do so. They also use one clerihew in each issue, for which they pay £15. (For those who, like me, wouldn't have known a clerihew from a limerick, a clerihew is a short witty poem usually consisting of two metrically irregular rhyming couplets.

Punch 23–27 Tudor Street, London EC4Y 0HR

Punch is, of course, a humorous magazine, edited by Alan Coren — himself no mean wit — and appearing weekly. If you can write really funny material, it could be a market worth investigating, but generally it is a hard one to break into. Much of the contents are written on commission by well-known humorists, but nevertheless, if you have an idea for a short (1200-word maximum), topical and witty article, then it is always worth sending it in, "on spec". If it does sell, the pay is good.

Spare Rib 27 Clerkenwell Close, London EC1R 0AT

Certainly, *Spare Rib* accepts freelance contributions, but it is a very specialized market to write for: you either can or you can't. The whole of the magazine is full of news stories, pictures and articles about the women's liberation movement. It is very much left-of-centre in its political stance and leans towards the "gay" side of the street. To write acceptable material for *Spare Rib* you would need to be "far out" liberated: if you are, you probably already know the magazine anyway; if you are not that liberated, don't try to write for them. *Spare Rib* is a monthly and costs 70p per copy.

City Limits 313 Upper Street, London N1 2XQ

City Limits is a weekly 60p magazine, full of listings of what's on in London, which take up nearly two-thirds of its 90-odd pages. The listings are very comprehensive, for films, theatre, etc., tending towards the more left-wing, "gay" and feminist happenings around town. There are some editorial pages but there are few opportunities for freelance writers to contribute; at first sight this is not obvious, but on closer inspection, many of the "freelance writers" turn out to be on the staff of the magazine. There is a lively letters page, but no payment is offered.

Time Out Tower House, Southampton Street, London WC2E 7HD

Another magazine listing what's on in London, *Time Out* is a weekly, selling at 60p. A typical issue contains over 100 pages of which no more than half a dozen are given over to feature articles — and these all appear to be commissioned. (Certainly they would require very "in" knowledge to write: not the sort of feature the "ordinary" freelance could produce.) The whole of the rest of the magazine is devoted to reviews and listings — plus a lot of advetisements. It is in fact almost exactly like one of the London free magazines, only more so, and somewhat left-of-centre in its political stance.

Cosmopolitan 72 Broadwick Street, London W1V 2BP
Company 72 Broadwick Street, London W1V 2BP
Options 27 Newman Street, London W1P 3PE

All three of Britain's most glossy, up-market magazines for the independent woman are poor markets for the freelance writer. They state quite clearly — albeit in the small print — that they are either not at all, or only barely, interested in unsolicited manuscripts. Marvellous magazines to read, but don't even dream of writing for them — wait for them to contact you, and don't hold your breath while waiting.

Signature Diners Club House, Kingsmead, Farnborough, Hants GU14 7SR

The magazine of Diners Club International, *Signature* has, in the past, been a good market for freelance contributions — and it paid very good rates. Diners Club has however been taken over by the New York company Citicorp, and this has meant a review of editorial policy. Currently the editor is not commissioning or accepting new material for the immediately foreseeable future. Watch this space.

Parents 116 Newgate Street, London EC1A 7AE

At first sight, *Parents* looks an ideal market for the young freelance writer-cum-parent; it uses articles giving advice to young parents and "how-to" features which most freelances could write. But the title page states bluntly, "We regret that we are unable to consider unsolicited material." However *Parents* welcomes ideas for subjects that readers would like it to cover. All published material is either staff-written or commissioned.

There is a letters page — but this too is of virtually no interest to the freelance writer; it does not pay for contributions, it just offers a £10 voucher for one "letter of the month".

Observer Magazine 8 St Andrew's Hill, London EC4V 5JA
Sunday Times Magazine 200 Gray's Inn Road, London WC1X 8EZ
Telegraph Sunday Magazine 135 Fleet Street, London EC4P 4BL

The Sunday colour-supplements do purchase articles from freelance writers — but almost always only as a result of editorial commissions. They all pay very high rates for acceptable work — around £100 per 1000 words and up — but their standards are very high indeed and the likelihood of the ordinary freelance breaking into this market is remote.

Watch out for their competitions, though. From time to time each of the magazines run competitions in travel writing, essay writing, humorous writing, and even short story writing. There are always excellent prizes — in the region of £1000. And they run photographic competitions too.

Mayfair 95a Chancery Lane, London WC2A 1DZ
Men Only 2 Archer Street, London W1V 7HE
Razzle 2 Archer Street, London W1V 7HE

The "soft (!) porn" men's magazines that offer highly erotic "girlie" pictures and unbelievable tales of sexual exploits are usually sold from the top shelf in the newsagents' shops. If you are willing to consider contributing to such magazines, and will do your own market study, you will discover that as well as the pictures there are often several "straight" feature articles. The pay is usually very high for the feature articles — often around £100 per 1000 words — but the standards too are very high, and the work is often commissioned.

There also seems to be a market for what could be called "porno confessions" — highly explicit first-person stories of sexual exploits. *Razzle* uses one 800-word "confession" from "one of our lady readers" in each isssue, and I can't believe these are other than fictional.

My apologies, but you will have to do your own market research for these magazines. But it could be a study worth doing.

National Daily Newspapers

Although many of the provincial daily newspapers are quite good markets for freelance contributions, the London national dailies are on the whole not. Some of the "quality newspapers" — *Telegraph* and *Guardian* rather than *Times* or *FT* — occasionally buy articles from "non-name" freelance writers (and see the market study report on *The Guardian*) but the tabloids seldom do. Some of the tabloids are however interested in hearing of ideas for their staff writers to investigate and write up — and will pay quite well just for the idea. So, if you feel someone, or some group of people, is being put upon, or is making an unjustifiable "killing", or has done something particularly interesting, write to your favourite tabloid editor and suggest he look into the idea.

Local Magazines ("Mudshire Life" etc.)
Specialist, Hobby and Trade Magazines ("The Widget Maker" etc)
Free Publications ("The Letterbox Gazette" etc.)

The above types of publication are almost always excellent markets for the freelance writer. As explained at the beginning of this book though, they are excluded from the market studies because they will be well known to those best able to contribute to them. But don't forget them.

5
Who Uses What?

It is of course, not possible to list, in any precise manner, the stories and articles that will attract the interest of an editor. Editors are often looking for something new, something that they haven't done before, that they think will particularly interest their readers. It is one of the tasks of the freelance writer to come up with new ideas that will spark off the editor's interest. That said though, there are broad categories of article subject which fall naturally into the areas of interest of different magazines. The table overleaf, general though the subjects may be, offers a general idea of which magazine is most likely to use articles on which subject.

Similarly, short stories intended for readers in a certain age bracket are often best written around characters of a similar one. It is therefore possible to suggest that a story about teenage love is best suited to one group of magazines and unlikely to sell to a magazine with a readership aged generally in the late 40s. The story market part of the table categorizes magazines generally by age groups.

WHO USES WHAT?

MAGAZINE	ARTICLE SUBJECTS											Poetry	SHORT STORIES							
	Animals	Collecting	Countryside	General Interest	Getting/keeping a mate	Houses and Homes	Money Matters	Personal Experiences	Profiles and Biographies	Things to do	Travel		13–17	Late Teens	Young 20s	25–35	35–45	Over 45	Unspecified age	Picture Stories
Amat. Gardening									●											
Amat. Photographer									●											
Animal Ways	●							●					○							
Animal World	●							●	●				○							
Annabel				●	●			●		●					○	○				
Busy Bees' News	●											□								
Cat World	●							●				□								
Choice		●	●					●		●	●									
Christian Herald		●	●	●		●					●								○	
Christian Woman								●	●							○	○	○		
Country				●				●	●											
Country Life		●	●	●		●		●				□								
The Countryman		●	●	●		●		●				□								
Country Quest			●	●				●												
Do It Yourself										●										
Evergreen		●	●	●		●		●				□								
Family Circle				●						●					○					
The Field		●	●	●		●														
Freelance Writing								●	●											
The Geographical									●		●									
Girl				●									○	○						○
Girl (about Town)					●		●	●	●											
Good Housekeeping				●		●		●									○			
The Guardian		●						●		●	●									
Heritage		●	●	●		●			●			□								
Home & Country	●			●																
Ideal Home						●														
Illus. London News		●				●			●											
Jackie					●					●			○							○
Just Seventeen					●									○						
The Lady	●	●	●	●		●		●	●		●	□								
Living							●			●										
London Calling					●			●	●			□								
London's Alt. Mag.			●								●									
Look Now					●										○					

98

MAGAZINE	ARTICLE SUBJECTS												SHORT STORIES							
	Animals	Collecting	Countryside	General Interest	Getting/keeping a mate	Houses and Homes	Money Matters	Personal Experiences	Profiles and Biographies	Things to do	Travel	Poetry	13–17	Late Teens	Young 20s	25–35	35–45	Over 45	Unspecified age	Picture Stories
Loving															○					
Midweek				●																
Mother								●	●						○					
Ms London								●			●									
My Story															○					
My Weekly				●				●				□			○					
19				●																
Nursery World										●										
Oh Boy!													○	○						○
Out of Town	●	●		●		●		●												
Over 21					●										○					
Patches					●								○	○						○
People's Friend				●								□						○	○	
Pract. Householder						●				●										
Reader's Digest								●												
Red Letter																○	○			
Romance															○	○				
Secrets																○	○			
SHE				●				●	●			□			○					
This England	●	●		●		●			●			□								
The Townswoman				●		●	●	●												
True Romances															○					
True Story															○					
Weekend	●			●				●							○				○	
The Weekly News								●												
Woman				●			●		●						○					
Woman and Home				●				●							○					
Woman's Journal				●				●									○			
Woman's Own				●				●												
Woman's Realm								●										○	○	
Woman's Story																			○	
Woman's Weekly															○					
Writer										●		□								
The Writer's Voice										●		□							○	
Writing										●		□								

6

Writing Photo-Story Scripts

Photo-story scripts offer an outlet for the fiction writer that is often overlooked. Both IPC and D.C. Thomson publish several weekly magazines filled with photo-stories; and both are very eager to purchase good scripts for these stories. Each picture-magazine uses 4 or 5 picture-stories each week and there are more than a handful of such magazines. In their usual helpful way, D.C. Thomson will provide interested writers with a whole sheaf of advice on their requirements and how best to meet these needs. (Write to Fiction Department — Photo-scripts, D.C. Thomson & Co. Ltd, Courier Buildings, Courier Place, Dundee DD1 9QJ.)

Photo-stories are just like any other form of fiction: they entail the use of all the customary story-telling skills — plus a few additional skills and techniques. Before studying the market in detail, it may help the starting writer to know some of the ground rules:

- The writer is not required — and indeed should not attempt — to provide the photographs for the story. All that is required from the writer is a script. Photo-stories are told in a specific number of pictured "frames"; for each frame the writer must provide all the details.
- Like any other work of fiction, the obvious and basic need is a good story. This needs — even more than usual — to have: a gripping opening, to grab the reader's interest; a strong, uncomplicated plot, complete with atmosphere and a small cast of really believable characters; and a good, powerful ending to the tale, tying up any loose ends.
- For each frame in the story, the writer must provide: a brief description of the scene portrayed, from which the photographer will work; the characters' necessary dialogue and thoughts (a particularly useful technique this) to be displayed in "balloons"; and any necessary captions.
- Speech, thoughts and captions alike should all be kept as brief as possible. There is no scope in a photo-story for a lengthy soliloquy; all speech and thoughts must carry the action forward. Any necessary descriptive material should be visible in the picture and therefore best left unsaid. It is a good idea to aim at a maximum length of speeches, thoughts and captions of no more than 25 words — and most should be

considerably shorter than that. Basically, the shorter the better.

- The personalities of the characters in the photo-story should be brought out through the dialogue, the thoughts and the action — not by lengthy descriptions. The captions should be restricted to no more than is necessary to perhaps replace a series of action-less pictures, or simply to establish the time — "Next morning".
- The description of the scene portrayed in each frame should similarly be kept brief — but for a different reason. It is best to allow the photographer to use his own imagination in setting the scene. He will fit the story to whatever he has that is suitable and readily available. The writer need only say, for instance, "Val is slumped on her bed, weeping." It is neither necessary nor desirable to describe the bedroom and its furniture; Val herself will already have been described.
- Restrict the number of characters and locations used: remember that each character photographed has to be paid for, and that each person has to be transported to each fresh location. Ensure too, that the characters are significantly different in appearance and that their names are not similar.
- Photo-story scripts should be typed on the customary A4 paper, in double-spacing. Allow a wide left margin: in that, type the frame number and alongside, provide the description; beneath that, type the speeches and thoughts, using the left margin again to identify the person speaking or thinking; and when necessary, type "caption" in the left margin and the words alongside. Restrict each page of A4 paper to no more than two frames.

7

Submissions to Editors — The Basic Principles

The ordinary freelance writer is in a buyers' market — he has to work at selling his stories and articles. And one of the things that every editor mentions about unsolicited work is the need for it to be "properly presented". The presentation of your work — how it looks when it lands on the the editor's desk — is of crucial importance; it is in effect, the "shop window" for your wares. There are certain basic principles about the presentation of work, and also generally about approaching editors. These principles — surely well known, but clearly in need of repetition — are:

- All work must be typed, on white A4 paper (297mm × 210mm) of about 70 gsm weight (not too thick, not too thin). For your own benefit, you need to retain a copy of your work, so use a sheet of carbon paper and thin "bank", 45gsm, A4 paper for the record.
- On the first page of a short story or article type your (real) name and address right up in the right-hand corner, in close spacing. Then scroll the paper down about one-third of the page and type the title, in capitals, centrally on the line; underline it and scroll down three or four single-spaced lines; now type your own name or your pen-name in lower case type, and underline that too. If you use a pen-name, you might like to type "Real name: Belinda Smith" in brackets, immediately below it — but this is optional.
- Beneath the title and your name, scroll down to about the centre of the sheet and begin your story or article. Throughout the manuscript, type on alternate lines — set the typewriter to scroll down two lines at a time — and indent the start of each paragraph by five spaces.
- Set the margins on the typewriter so that you leave about 20 spaces at the left of the page and perhaps 12 to 15 on the right. Put another way, you need margins of about two inches (40 – 50mm) on the left and one inch (25mm) on the right. These wide margins are to provide room for the editor to make corrections and give instructions to the printers.
- Stop typing at least an inch (25mm), and preferably more, from the foot of the page. Try to avoid carrying over a "widow" — half a line or less to the end of the paragraph — onto the next page.
- At the top of page 2 and all other pages, provide the "strap" — the

manuscript identification — which should be something like "Wells/ Title/2", either spread across the top line and underlined, or just in the top right corner. The "Title" should not be the full title but merely one, or at most two, significant words from it. Leave a blank line between the "strap" and the first line of the text proper.

- For articles, I prefer to leave a double double-space between paragraphs; for short stories this is not desirable.

- When you get to the end of your story or article, scroll down another couple of lines and type a short row of dots in the centre of the page followed by, in capitals, the word "END". Then scroll the paper down to the bottom and in the bottom left-hand corner, type your (real) name and address again, single-spaced.

- A cover page is a good idea. It is not universally recommended but I have always found it worth doing; it is sometimes removed in the editorial offices and sent to the accounts section as the basis of payment. The title page should repeat the title in the centre of the page, with the real or pen-name centred below it. Below the title you should say how many words there are in the manuscript, and — for illustrated articles — how many pictures accompany it. Your (real) name and address should be typed at the bottom left of the cover page and, for stories, type "FBSR (First British Serial Rights) offered" in either the top or the bottom right corner. (I do not consider it necessary to include this identification of rights offered when submitting an article in Britain; it is always assumed. This is not the case when submitting articles to American magazines though.)

- If you are submitting an illustrated article, you need to include the captions for the pictures. I like to provide these on a separate caption sheet which I attach to the back of the manuscript. Some editors, however, like the captions attached to the back of the illustrations. If you provide a caption sheet, ensure that the pictures have an identification letter or number on the back to relate to the captions.

- I believe in sending a brief covering letter with every manuscript. (Many freelance writers do not — I think they are wrong, as long as the letter is brief.) The letter need only say, effectively, "Here is an article/story about. . . . If you like it please pay; if you don't, please return." A letter looks businesslike. And if you have any particular qualifications for writing a feature, this is the place to tell the editor so — BRIEFLY.

- If the manuscript (story or article) is less than about 1500 words in length and unillustrated, then I would fold it twice to fit into a 9 inch by 4½ inch (DL size) envelope. If longer and unillustrated, I would merely fold it in half. If illustrated, clearly the photographs cannot be folded, and must be protected with a sheet of cardboard — which will probably mean a large, A4-size, envelope. Always enclose a ready-stamped self-addressed return envelope — of the appropriate size — with every unsolicited submission or query sent to an editor.

- In my view, it is seldom necessary, when submitting manuscripts of less than about 1500 words to editors in Britain, to send a prior query. One or two British editors prefer queries but quite often the query will need to be a synopsis, which will need nearly as much work as the full — short — article; and a query will double your postage costs. Without doubt, queries are wise for longer articles and are usually essential for American magazines. They are almost never necessary for short stories.
- And the most basic principle of all: write for a market. Don't write a story or article and then look around for a suitable magazine to submit it to. The story-line needs of different magazines vary widely; different magazines want different approaches in their features too. And the way to ensure that you hit the target is first to read this handbook, and then, having selected a few target magazines, to study these in even greater detail. When you really know the magazine it is easier to produce suitable material for it. And — initially, at least — concentrate on just a few magazines.

8
Getting Together

Writing is a lonely occupation; it is not a pastime for two. You alone can commune with that blank page in front of you. But writers can undoubtedly benefit from the company of other writers — for limited periods. Many people, when starting to write, are unaware of the opportunities there are for getting together with others at a similar stage in their writing development. There are many such opportunities.

Writers can get together at writers' circles — there are such circles of enthusiasts throughout the country — at writers' schools and conferences, and through the pages of the several small writing magazines.

Writers' Circles

There is an excellent directory of just about every writers' circle in the country, that has been compiled by journalist Jill Dick. This booklet is available from Laurence Pollinger Ltd, 18 Maddox Street, London W1R 0EU, for under £2. (The price is inevitably increasing but a blank cheque "limited to not more than £3" should cover cost and postage.)

Some of the larger writers' circles however can be contacted through the following people:

London Writer Circle, c/o Marjorie Harris, 37 Manor Farm Road, Bitterne Park, Southampton SO9 3FQ.

Birmingham Writers' Group, c/o Victoria Oakley, Flat 34, Halifax House, Bristol Road, Edgbaston, Birmingham B5 7XU.

Croydon Writers' Circle, c/o Daphne Moss, 12 Park Road, Beckenham, Kent BR3 1QD.

Dorking Writers' Circle, c/o Lucia White, 91 Dorking Road, Epsom, Surrey KT18 7JZ.

Leeds Writers' Circle, c/o Mary Pedley, 32 Sandringham Crescent, Shadwell, Leeds, West Yorks LS17 8DF.

Leicester Writers' Circle, c/o April Arnachellum, 35 Westfield Road, Leicester LE3 6HT.

Liverpool Writers' Club, c/o Joyce Nimmo, 72 Ampthill Road, Liverpool 17.

Nottingham Writers' Club, c/o Jean Trippett, 52 Hilton Road, Mapperley, Nottingham.

Scarborough Writers' Circle, c/o Hazel Michael, 2 Cromwell Terrace, Scarborough, North Yorks YO11 2DT.

Sheffield Writers' Club, c/o Mrs J. Board, 34 Lime Tree Avenue, Retford, Notts DN22 7BA.

The above clubs and circles are only a few of the hundreds that there are throughout the country. There are several ways of getting in touch with the circle nearest to your home: ask at your local library, they will probably know of the local club; contact one of the people listed above, they will possibly know of other clubs nearer to you; or buy a copy of Jill Dick's directory for a much more complete listing.

Courses: "Creative Writing"/"Writing for Pleasure and Profit"

Throughout the country Local Education Authorities or WEA committees organize evening courses in writing. Once again, the best first contact is your local library. The quality of the evening courses will of course vary with the tutor — but most are dedicated to their task of bringing out new talent. It is worth investigating the evening-class opportunities in your area.

The Writers' Summer School — Swanwick

The 5-day annual Writers' Summer School, held during August each year at The Hayes Conference Centre, Swanwick, Derbyshire, is the oldest-established of the writers' conferences. The first "Swanwick", as it is popularly known, was held in 1949 and it has been held annually in the same place ever since. It is by far the most popular conference and it is always a gamble whether one can get in; each year there are over 900 applications for just over 300 places.

A Swanwick conference starts at tea-time on the Saturday when the members begin to arrive and greet each other like long-lost cousins. From that moment on the talking never stops — new members are advised to invest in ear-plugs. There is a welcoming "assembly" on the Saturday evening and the "school" proper starts on the Sunday morning at 9.30 with the first of 10 formal lectures. The major lectures are given by leading figures in the writing and publishing world; the list of those who have spoken at Swanwick would be virtually a writers' Who's Who.

Apart from the formal lectures there are usually 5 or 6 courses in various types of writing. There is always a course for beginner writers, there is usually one on short-story writing and one on some form of novel-writing. There is usually one too on some form of non-fiction writing — articles or books. Other courses vary from year to year.

As well as the courses, which comprise three or more linked talks, often with "homework" to be done between talks, there are dozens of talks and discussion groups running concurrently, all day long. Members of the Swanwick school usually have a choice of 4 or 5 different talks going on at any time. The writer who cannot find something of interest at any hour of the day — talk, lecture, discussion, or just chatting to fellow writers in the bar — must be very hard to please. The Swanwick day starts at 9.30 am and the last talk may not finish until nearly 11 pm — and there is dancing after that until 1 am almost every night.

To get to Swanwick, you need first to get an application form. Write to The Secretary, Philippa Boland, at The Red House, Mardens Hill, Crowborough, East Sussex TN6 1XN, before Christmas in the year before you hope to attend. Send her a long (DL size) stamped addressed envelope and wait. Around the end of January or early February the form will arrive. It is then important to quickly complete and despatch the form, together with a cheque for the full cost, currently £80 but increasing every year. (The cost covers full board and lodging from Saturday teatime to Friday morning, and all lectures and courses — the lot.) If you do not return the application form immediately, your chances of acceptance are very slight. (There are stories of Swanwick-addicts driving to the main post office to despatch their application form and cheque — still wearing their dressing gowns!)

The form despatched, all you can do is cross your fingers and wait. By about the middle of February you will get a receipt — or your money back. Then in July details of the programme and joining instructions will arrive. You are all set for a stimulating week.

Writers' Conferences

Other than Swanwick, there are major weekend conferences each year at three other venues: Cardiff, Scarborough and Chichester. Each has a charm and character of its own.

There are two weekend conferences each year at both Scarborough and Cardiff, both are late and early in the year; the once-yearly Southern Writers' Conference at Earnley Concourse, near Chichester is held in mid-June. Each of the weekend conferences run from Friday teatime to Sunday teatime; each is well filled with formal lectures and with tutorial and/or discussion groups; each provides time for getting to know other writers socially — and talking shop into the small hours.

A place at the weekend conferences is not at quite such a premium as at Swanwick — nevertheless, to be sure of a place it is always essential to book early. (Places for the Scarborough weekends are in fact at such a premium that attendance there is by invitation only!) It is probably best to enquire about all of the next year's conferences before Christmas — and always send a DL-sized stamped addressed envelope. Organizers and approximate dates and costs of the weekends are:

Southern Writers' Conference: Joy Peach, 31 North View, Winchester, Hants. Held in mid-June and offering 5 or 6 top speakers plus about a dozen workshop/tutorials in four concurrent streams, there are around 90 places at approximately £60 per head; accommodation is in a very comfortable purpose-made residential conference centre, The Earnley Concourse, by the seaside, south of Chichester, West Sussex

Scarborough Writers' Weekends: Audrey Wilson, The Firs, Filey Road, Osgodby, Scarborough, N. Yorks YO11 3NH. The Scarborough weekends are held in April and November: the April weekend offers 4 or 5 top speakers and a dozen or so discussion groups; the November weekend is all discussion groups — nearly 30 of them, in four streams. Places at Scarborough are at a premium, and demand always outstrips supply: only 100 people can be accommodated in the convenient and comfortable hotel; the weekend costs approximately £45 per head and places are by invitation only — but it might be worth asking, the weekends have a great reputation.

The South and Mid-Wales Association of Writers' (SAMWAW) Weekend Courses: Marguerite Prisk, 48 Baron Road, Penarth, South Glamorgan, Wales CF6 1UE. The SAMWAW weekends are held in May and September each year at the beautiful Dyffryn House Conference Centre, just outside of Cardiff (a mini-bus meets the London train). In May, there are two major evening lectures, and then each of four tutors, working in two concurrent streams, talks to and chairs two long sessions of discussion about a particular writing specialism. In September the weekend is mainly given over to two in-depth study courses; on both weekends there are, of course, other activities — including an evening "entertainment". At present the SAMWAW weekends cost about £45 — the accommodation is all in very comfortable single rooms.

Writing magazines

The are now 5 small quarterly writers' magazines on sale in Britain; 4 of these pay for contributions — albeit very small payment — and are therefore included in the market-study pages of this book. These paying magazines are *Freelance Writing* (and Photography), *The Writers' Voice*, *Writer*, and *Writing* — and their value to the ordinary freelance magazine writer is probably in just about that order.

The other small magazine is a reduced-size typewritten one called *Success*, which does not pay for contributions but offers postal "workshop" facilities within the subscription. *Success* is friendly and very personal — almost like belonging to a club. The articles are often very helpful, and are written by "ordinary" writers about "ordinary" problems. They are never over the beginner writer's head.

Success is available for £5.50 per year from Kate Dean, 17 Andrews Crescent, Peterborough PE4 6XL; a free sample copy is available for a first-class stamp.

Every spare-time freelance writer will get something of value from at least one of the writers' magazines — if only just to keep in touch with what is going on in the rest of the writing world.

There is one further writers' publication that demands to be mentioned and this is the *Contributor's Bulletin*, published 11 times a year by Freelance Press Services, 5/9 Bexley Square, Manchester M3 6DB. A subscription costs £11.85 for 11 issues — and this can easily be re-earned from just one item of market information in the first issue of a subscription.

Each issue of the *Contributor's Bulletin* contains up-dating market information on a wide variety of magazines — many of very narrow interest — but there are always one or two items of interest to every individual reader. It could be thought of as the monthly supplement to *The Magazine Writers' Handbook*. A subscription is strongly recommended.

NOTE: A new, monthly writers' magazine, *Writers' Monthly*, has recently been launched. A very professionally produced A4-sized magazine, it is available on subscription from The Writer Ltd, P.O. Box 34, St Andrews, Fife, Scotland KY16 9RH.

9
Competitions

No "ordinary" spare-time writer — particularly of short stories or poetry — can afford to ignore competitions. They are often the only way that a perhaps slightly adventurous poet can get his work into print. And the rewards for some of the competitions are not to be overlooked. Not for the ordinary writer the fame and fortune of the Booker or Trask awards however — these require a full-length novel, and for the Booker Prize, a published one at that. Spare-time writers' prizes are measured in hundreds of pounds — and less.

Short Story Competitions

There are not many regular short-story competitions — but there are quite a lot of one-off ones. It is up to the writer to find out about the short-story competitions as and when they are announced. It is not uncommon for women's magazines to organize short-story competitions; for a year or so — but now no longer — *Woman's Own* magazine ran an annual short-story competition. Not only did they reward and publish the winning entries, but they also bought all other stories that were worth publishing, meeting their whole fiction needs in this way.

The way to keep aware of one-off competitions is to follow the reports in *Contributors Bulletin*. (Details see "Getting Together".) And of course, to keep an eye on likely magazines for oneself. Magazines and organizations that have run short-story competitions in recent years have included: *Woman's Realm*, *Fiction Magazine*, *The New Writer*, the *Telegraph Sunday Magazine*, Websters Book Shops, *TV Times*, the Isle of Wight Writers' Circle (in association with the IOW County Press), the Fellowship of Christian Writers, and Lion Books with *Buzz* magazine. The opportunities are many and varied.

There are however, a few regular, established, short-story competitions. Details of these are given below. In all cases, a stamped self-addressed envelope should be sent when seeking details.

The Catherine Cookson Cup Competition: organized annually by the Hastings Writers' Group. Entry forms and details are obtainable from the competition secretary, Mrs Mary F. Monk, 70 Lower Park Road, Hastings, East Sussex. The short stories are required to be no longer than 2500 words; the closing date is usually at the end of August. The cup, donated by the well-known author of best-selling romances, together with a first prize of £100, is presented annually, at a winter social event in Sussex. Second and third prizes are £50 and £25.

The H.E. Bates Short-Story Competition: organized annually by the Tourist Information Centre, 21 St Giles Street, Northampton, from whom details and entry forms can be obtained. The short story must be no longer than 2000 words in length; the first prize is £50 and other prizes are worth a total of another £50.

The Cecil Hunt Scholarship: organized by the magazine *Competitor's Journal*, P.O. Box 94, London W4 2ER. The main prize is a free — and certain — place at that year's Writers' Summer School at Swanwick. (See "Getting Together", page 105, for more information about Swanwick.) The second prize is £5. Entry to the competition is restricted to those who have not previously attended the school. The story is required not to exceed 2000 words, the subject is set afresh each year; the closing date is usually at the end of April.

The Crediton Writers' Circle Short-Story Competition: this has been organized for some years now by the Writers' Circle; there is also a poetry competition run by the same club (see below). For details write to Mrs M. Finch, "Bramblings", Searle Street, Crediton, Devon EX17 3DB. Competitors can submit as many stories as they like, each not exceeding 1500 words, on any theme, each accompanied by a £1 entry fee. First prize is £100, second prize £50, third £25, and there are five more prizes of £5 each for the runners-up. Closing date is usually around the end of March each year.

Magazine Competitions: short-story and poetry competitions are a regular feature of many of the writing and other small-circulation magazines. *Success*, *The Writer's Voice*, *Writer*, *The New Writer* and *London Calling*, all have such competitions running regularly. The prizes are not often large, but the *Writer's Voice* offers £50 and £25 and *The New Writer* offers £75 and £35, which are good. (The address of *The New Writer* is Five Ash Lane, Sutton Veny, Wilts, BA12 7BH. For addresses of other magazines see elsewhere in the text.) To enter the magazine competitions it is usually necessary to be a subscriber — but this is often worthwhile anyway.

Poetry Competitions

Perhaps to make up for the dearth of opportunities for unsolicited submissions to most magazines, there are a good number of literary competitions for poets — and for some, the prizes are good.

National Poetry Competition: organized by the Poetry Society, this is the biggest and best of all. The first prize is £2000, the second £1000 and the third £500; and there are 5 consolation prizes of £100, ten of £50 and a big bundle of £10 poetry book-vouchers. Details of the Competition can be obtained from the Competition Organizer, National Poetry Centre, 21 Earl's Court Square, London SW5 9DE. Poems may be on any subject, must be in English, must not be more than 40 lines in length and up to 10 poems may be submitted by any one competitor — each accompanied by the entry fee of £1.50. Closing date is usually at the beginning of November each year. The judges are highly prestigious.

Leek Arts Festival Poetry Competition: this has been running for several years now; the organizer is Roger Elkin, 44 Rudyard Road, Biddulph Moor, Stoke-on-Trent, Staffs ST8 7JN, from whom full details can be obtained. Prizes for this contest are £150, £100 and £50.

Arvon Foundation Competitions: poetry competitions are regularly held by the Arvon Foundation; they will put interested people on their mailing list for details of future competitions. Write to Arvon Foundation, Kilnhurst Road, Todmorden, Lancashire OL14 6AX.

Salopian Open Poetry Competition: organized for several years now by the Salopian Poetry Society; the organizer is Mr S. Yapp, 6 Avondale, Lawley Bank, Telford, Shropshire TF4 2LW. Prizes are small, £12, £6 and £4 with three runners-up prizes of £2 each.

Crediton Writers' Circle Poetry Competition: details as for the short story competition above. Prizes are £50, £25 and £10; entry fee is 50p; closing date is at the end of March.

Magazine Competitions: as mentioned above, most of the writing and some other small magazines organize poetry competitions. *Success* is consistently the best of the small writing magazines for poetry. They publish a book of poems each year and the magazine is always half-full of poems. *The Writer's Voice* however offers bigger prizes.

10

Addresses Useful to the Freelance Writer

The freelance non-fiction writer depends on information — and personal experience — to keep him writing. And, as mentioned in "Getting Together" he can benefit from associating with other writers.

In this section of the Handbook are listed some useful addresses for acquiring information or for associating with other writers. (These latter associations are of less general application than those dealt with, in more detail, in the earlier chapter.)

Press Cuttings

No, not the agencies that give you all the reviews of your latest book, but an agency that will provide you with a batch of newspaper cuttings collected over a period of some years, all on a single subject. (At one time, I obtained about 20 or so cuttings all dealing with unusual hats; this provided part of the material for an article I wrote on hats.) Write to: Mrs P. Kenderdine, 65 Cambridge Road, Linthorpe, Middlesbrough, Cleveland TS5 5NL. Unfortunately Mrs Kenderdine cannot supply lists of the subjects that she has cuttings about — but ask her for almost anything and she may be able to help. Stamped addressed envelope for a reply, of course. She charges about £1 per set of cuttings.

Associations

Fellowship of Christian Writers. Contact: Mrs Joan Garwood, 104 Evelyn Street, London SE8 5DD.

Society of Authors. (Join when you have written a book and a publisher has accepted it, but before you sign the contract.) Address: 84 Drayton Gardens, London SW10 9SB.

Society of Women Writers and Journalists. (Just what its name implies.) Contact: SWWJ, c/o Old Fyning House, Rogate, Petersfield, Hants GU31 5EF.

Major Government Offices of Interest in London

For all major government departments, write to The Information Officer, and in these days of austerity, it is probably best to enclose a stamped addressed envelope for reply.

Ministry of Agriculture, Fisheries & Food, Whitehall Place, London SW1.

Central Office of Information, Hercules Road, London SE1.

Department of Education & Science, Elizabeth House, York Road, London SE1.

Department of the Environment, 2 Marsham Street, London SW1.

Department of Health and Social Security, Alexander Fleming House, Elephant and Castle, London SE1.

Home Office, 50 Queen Anne's Gate, London SW1.

Department of Trade & Industry, 1–19 Victoria Street, London SW1.

Department of Transport, 2 Marsham Street, London SW1.

HM Treasury, Parliament Street, London SW1.

Major Foreign Embassies in London

American Embassy, 24 Grosvenor Square, London W1.

Australian High Commission, Australia House, Strand, London WC2.

Canadian High Commission, Macdonald House, 1 Grosvenor Square, London W1.

Chinese Embassy, 31 Portland Place, London W1.

French Embassy, 58 Knightsbridge, London SW1.

German Embassy of the Federal Republic of Germany, 23 Belgrave Square, London SW1.

High Commissioner for India, India House, Aldwych, London WC2.

Italian Embassy, 14 Three Kings Yard, London W1.

Japanese Embassy, 46 Grosvenor Street, London W1.

Netherlands Embassy, 38 Hyde Park Gate, London SW7.

High Commissioner for New Zealand, New Zealand House, Haymarket, London SW1.

Nigeria High Commission, Nigeria House, 9 Northumberland Avenue, London WC2.

South African Embassy, South Africa House, Trafalgar Square, London WC2.

Soviet Embassy, 18 Kensington Palace Gardens, London W8.

Swedish Embassy, 11 Montagu Place, London W1.

The above is a highly selective list of embassies and the like; for the addresses of other embassies, consult the London Telephone Directory, Yellow Pages, in your local public library. Don't forget also that all the major airlines have brochures about their home territory and the countries they visit; they may well be able, and willing, to provide the writer with useful information, and publicity photographs.

Major London Museums

In all cases, write initially to the Curator, and as above, in the present economic climate it is prudent to enclose a stamped addressed envelope.

Bethnal Green Museum (dolls), Cambridge Heath Road, London E2.
British Museum, Great Russell Street, London WC1.
Geological Museum (geology), Exhibition Road, South Kensington, London SW7.
Horniman Museum (people), London Road, Forest Hill, London SE23.
Imperial War Museum, Lambeth Road, London SE1.
National Army Museum, Royal Hospital Road, Chelsea, London SW3.
National Maritime Museum, Romney Road, Greenwich, London SE10.
National Postal Museum, King Edward Street, London EC1.
Natural History Museum, Cromwell Road, South Kensington, London SW7.
Public Record Office Museum, Chancery Lane, London WC2A.
Rotunda Museum (guns), Woolwich Common, London SE18.
Science Museum, Exhibition Road, South Kensington, London SW7.
Victoria & Albert Museum, Cromwell Road, South Kensington, London SW7.
William Morris Gallery, Lloyd Park, Walthamstow, London E17.

11

The Magazine Writer's Bookshelf

It is always difficult to recommend books for others; other people's needs and tastes are never the same as one's own. Nevertheless, there are some books associated with or about the business of writing for magazines that are fairly standard in their acceptance; and there are others that — at least in my view — are worth looking at. On these pages I list the books that I feel are useful: there are certainly others; some may be better for you.

Standard Reference Books

The Concise Oxford Dictionary (OUP). Many find it too academic but it is the one that I find easy to work with.

The Oxford Dictionary for Writers and Editors (OUP). Very useful for sorting out alternative spellings and telling you when to use capital letters, etc.

Roget's Thesaurus (available in Penguin). Good to refer to, but avoid the pitfalls of over-use.

The Penguin Encyclopedia (Penguin). A "first source" one-volume encyclopedia that often saves a longer search.

Everyman's Encylopedia (J.M. Dent). The original twelve-volume edition was expensive. It is now available in a much cheaper edition of six jumbo-sized volumes for under £100. Marvellous, at that price.

Ann Hoffmann: *Research* (A. & C. Black). An invaluable guide to hosts of research sources.

Annual Reference Books

The Writers' & Artists' Yearbook (A. & C. Black, annually). Covers an immense field of publications and publishers — and therefore with considerably less of the important details than this handbook — an essential overall reference.

The Writer's Yearbook (Writer's Digest, USA). A magazine-like publication listing and ranking the top 100 US magazine markets. It costs less than a fifth of the more comprehensive — and therefore better, but possibly not necessary — *Writer's Market*, also from Writer's Digest, which lists several thousand US markets.

Writing for Magazines

Dorothea Brande: *Becoming a Writer* (Papermac). I do not, myself, like this book — but everyone else does, so I'm probably wrong.

Brinig & Woudhuysen: *Breaking Into Print* (Wildwood House). An excellent but brief, market-orientated, "how to" book — fiction and non-fiction.

Mary T. Dillon: *Magazine Article Writing* (The Writer Inc.). Quite a helpful American book, if a shade pedestrian.

Gary Disher: *Writing Fiction* (Penguin). A slim book by an Australian writer — but it "travels well" and is of universal application.

Dianne Doubtfire: *Creative Writing* (Teach Yourself Books, Hodder & Stoughton). A superb textbook — starting from scratch — on the whole of the writing business, short stories, articles, books, plays, etc.

Gordon Wells: *The Craft of Writing Articles* (Allison & Busby). I think it's great — but I'm prejudiced. See for yourself.

L. Perry Wilbur: *How to Write Articles that Sell* (John Wiley & Sons). A down-to-earth, hard-selling, American guide to article-writing.

Handbook of Short Story Writing (Writer's Digest). A collection of hard-hitting American advice articles reprinted from *The Writer's Digest*. Useful; particularly for its variety of viewpoints.

Writing Style

Sir Ernest Gowers: *The Complete Plain Words* (HMSO). Good, if now slightly pedantic.

Robert Gunning: *The Technique of Clear Writing* (McGraw-Hill). Written mainly for the businessman, it nevertheless has a lot of advice of equal relevance to magazine writers.

Keith Waterhouse: *Daily Mirror Style* (Mirror Books). Easy reading — good solid advice — worth its weight in gold.

And finally, Technology

Ray Hammond: *The Writer and the Word Processor* (Coronet). A marvellous new (November 1984) paperback book, that explains, specifically for writers, all you need to know about the word processor.

12

Word Processing for Writers

Hardly a day goes by without a press announcement of the launch of a new home computer, often "complete with word processor". Business magazines and television commercials promote the world of "Information Technology". The word processor is with us; we cannot escape from it; we must learn to live with it.

So . . . what is a word processor? Basically, a word processor is a computerized typewriter, with which you write directly onto a screen. But it is more than just that. It is a whole new approach to writing. It involves a completely new set of techniques that, once mastered, make life far easier for the writer. And, just recently, with the rapid developments in home computing, it has come within the financial grasp of many ordinary writers.

A few years ago I enquired about the cost of a word processor; I was quoted £7500 — and promptly stopped asking. Only a couple of years ago I asked again — and was told that I could build myself a good one for £1500; this was still outside my limit. I have now bought one — on which the whole of this book was written — at a cost of just over £700 (see details below).

A word processor is a device whereby you can type on a reasonably normal typewriter keyboard; see your words appearing immediately in front of you on a television-like screen; correct them to your complete satisfaction; and then be able to print them out at will on ordinary typing paper. The word processor means being able to draft directly onto the typewriter. It means being able to correct and polish until satisfied, and then to produce a final perfectly typed top copy in minutes. (But in the world of word processors, nothing is ever quite final before its despatch to the editor; it is so easy to make corrections, and a new top copy is only the press of a button away.)

There are two types of word processor: the "dedicated" processor — a small computer designed solely to process words, and often with all of the constituent parts in a single console; and the small home computer which, with peripheral equipment, is capable of operating as a word processor.

The first type is still expensive and is strictly limited in its uses — but it is very easy to use; the second type is much cheaper, and may prove to have other uses beyond merely processing your words. (You could, for instance, use your computer not only for writing, but also to keep your writing accounts, to hold your files of editors' names and addresses, and to keep records of which piece of work has been considered by which editor.) But the small home-computer is designed to be used as a computer — to play "arcade" games, etc. There will be a few minor snags in using it as a professional word processor — but they are very minor. (Occasionally, I have to address my computer in computer language — but this entails using only a very few short standardized phrases, such as "LRUN MDV1-BOOT" in order to start up. LRUN means "load and run the program", MDV1 is where the program is, and I have no idea why I have to use the word "BOOT" — but it seems to be a standard computing expression.)

In order to operate a home computer as a word processor, you will need several pieces of equipment. In summary first, these are:

- a computer with a reasonable keyboard,
- a monitor screen — like a TV screen but purpose built,
- an electronic means of storing your work,
- a printer to transfer your electronic words to paper,
- a set of instructions — a program — to make the computer work.

And you will need several special cables to join these various pieces of equipment together. (And getting the right cables is a bigger problem than it might at first appear.)

The Computer

Consider first the computer. Most home computers contain all of their electronic wizardry inside what looks like the front half of a typewriter — the keyboard without the platen and printing keys. There are many such home computers available — and the first thing that a writer needs to check is the keyboard itself. We have all learnt to type on the standard QWERTY keyboard, with keys that register positively to the touch. Some computers have a non-standard (and therefore unacceptable) keyboard, and some have "membrane" keyboards — electronic touch keys that are almost impossible to type on. Avoid these at all costs.

You also need to check that the computer has output sockets to enable a printer to be linked to it, and what sort. (What use is a word processor that can't print the words onto paper?) Ensure that the printer output socket on the computer is one of the standard ones, either RS–232 "serial" or Centronics "parallel". (See below.)

The next thing you will need to know about your computer is its (electronic) size. Inside the box of the computer are various electronic "chips" that make it work; most of this is of little importance to the writer — except for the size of the Random Access Memory (the RAM). The RAM is the part of the computer which not only holds your words (while you are working on them) but also the instructions to the computer to process the words. Many word processing programs — see below — take up a lot of the computer's storage space, leaving little room for your work in progress; this means that you would need to remove and store your work elsewhere more frequently than is convenient. Basically, you need a large RAM — at least 64K size — the bigger the better.

Information is held inside a computer in the form of electronic signals. Effectively, each letter, space, or other characer is one piece of information — and in computer jargon is known as a "byte". The average word, plus the space around it, is therefore about 8 to 10 bytes long (call it 10 bytes for convenience.) Computer storage is measured in bytes and to avoid long numbers the unit of measurement is 1024 bytes — which in round figures is 1000 bytes — known as one kilobyte, or just 1K. (Similarly, a megabyte or 1M is a million bytes.) If therefore a computer has an in-built storage capacity, or RAM, of 64K bytes, this means that it can contain 64,000 bytes of information — or roughly 6400 words. (But remember, some of the storage space is needed for the word processor program itself, to make the computer work.) So . . . the bigger the RAM, the more useful the home computer to the writer.

The Monitor

The next essential part of the home computer word processor set-up is a screen on which to see what you are writing. When a home computer is used for the usual "arcade" games, a TV screen is sufficient for the display. But a television set is not designed to display a lot of fine detail in the form of small printed characters. Using a TV screen linked to a home computer usually limits the number of readable characters across the screen to 40. Most of us writers need at least 60, and preferably 80 characters of usable screen width. To get this facility you will need a monitor, or Visual Display Unit (VDU).

Monitors are just like TV screens but are designed to give higher resolution, to display 80 characters across the screen width. Monitors, like TV screens, can be full-colour or monochrome. For the writer, using his home computer almost entirely as a word processor, a monochrome screen is perfectly adequate; indeed, it is arguably better than a colour monitor. (The colours are not necessary, cost money, and can distract.) Monochrome monitors usually have either a green or a bronze screen rather than black and white — the colours being more restful on the eyes.

Once you have written your well-chosen words onto the screen, you will inevitably discover that you wish to change them. Careful editing of one's writing is an essential part of the polishing process that changes mere scribbles into saleable prose. Using a word processor, the writer can get his work as near perfect as possible before printing it out.

But you may not be able — or wish — to both write and finally polish your work in a single session. The word processor enables you to store the unpolished work and then recall it to the screen at your later convenience for editing, rewriting, or final polishing. Or you can print out a rough draft, correct it, and then transfer just the corrections to the work previously stored.

The Storage

In some cheaper home computers, cassette tape recorders are used as the storage device. An ordinary tape cassette can hold and "play" electronic signals which the computer reads as instructions on word processing; the cassette will also accept and store electronic signals representing the word that you type into the computer. But cassette recorders are very very slow as computer storage devices. The computer has to read right through the tape to find any single piece of information that may be needed.

The best way of storing information from and for the computer is undoubtedly on what are called "floppy discs" — or just "floppies". These are small, approximately 3″ or 5″ diameter plastic discs, not unlike records, which can be read by an electronic scanner in random order. In other words, the scanner can extract information virtually immediately, from anywhere on the floppy disc.

Many word-processing programs ("software" — see below) are supplied directly on a floppy disc. To use these programs a disc drive (like a record player with an electronic scanner), and preferably a double disc drive, is needed. The disc drive has to be linked to the computer so that the instructions on the disc can be read into the RAM, and so that the words you write on the computer screen can be "saved" onto the storage disc. Typically, a 5″ floppy can store about 300K bytes of information.

There is a half-way house in storage devices. The Sinclair computers, and notably the QL (see below), operate with what are called Microdrives and Microdrive cartridges. The Microdrive cartridges used by Sinclair contain a 200-inch-long continuous loop of high quality electronic (video) tape which runs past a reading head at 28 inches per second — far faster than an ordinary cassette tape. Because of the high running speed and the continuous loop, the Microdrive cartridges provide a very fast access to anywhere on the spool of tape. They are not as good as floppy discs and disc drives, but they are a practical, and cheaper, alternative. A Sinclair Microdrive cartridge can store approximately 100K bytes — 4 or 5 short stories or articles.

The Printer

The next, and essential, part of the word processing system for writers that can be built around a home computer is the printer. There are two

121

types of printer: the dot-matrix and the daisy-wheel. The dot-matrix printer marks the paper in a fine pattern of dots in the shape of the character; the daisy-wheel printer strikes the page with a full character just like a conventional typewriter.

The dot-matrix printer has a set of fine pins that are caused to project through a matrix of holes, perhaps 9 × 9; in the shape of the required character. The pins press against the ribbon and onto the paper producing the character. A poor-quality dot-matrix printer — as often used for computer print-out or for mail-order address labels — is not always easy to read. A good-quality dot-matrix printer can produce what is called "near letter quality" typescript — but this quality is expensive, and is not always quite so "near" as is claimed. In America, where the use of word processors by writers is more prevalent than in Britain, some editors will not even consider work presented to them that has been produced on a dot-matrix machine. Not all editors are so fussy and in time they may come to accept good dot-matrix work, but for the present, magazine writers would be well advised to select a daisy-wheel printer.

Daisy-wheel printers are far slower operating than are dot-matrix printers. Many dot-matrix printers operate at 80 characters per second (cps); the average daisy-wheel printer operates at less than 20 characters per second.

A daisy-wheel printer is much like an electronic typewriter without the keyboard — but it also contains an electronic device which accepts instructions from the computer about what to print. Mechanically, there are a set of tiny arms, each with a character embossed upon the tip, which are arranged — like the petals of a daisy — around a central hub. The wheel spins, the correct character is locked in position, a tiny hammer strikes the tip of the arm or petal, which in turn hits the typewriter ribbon onto the paper, and a letter is printed.

Both types of printer can be obtained with the means of accepting continuous rolls, or folds, of paper. For the writer, with the slower-operating daisy-wheel printer, this is hardly necessary; it is not difficult to insert a fresh sheet of paper every two or three minutes. With a dot-matrix printer however, pages speed through very quickly and continuous-feed paper may be an advantage.

Just as, when selecting a computer, it was necessary to consider its compatibility with a printer, so too, when selecting a printer, must compatibility be considered. Some computers will only permit "serial" connection to a printer; others only "parallel" connection. The terms are of little importance: a serial connection means that information is fed "down the wire" one item after the other; a parallel connection permits information to be transmitted in blocks. (Serial connections are also known as RS–232 interfaces, while parallel connections can be referred to as Centronics.) Few printers will allow both serial and parallel operation; most will be one or the other; some can have the type of connection specified at purchase. Ascertain the requirements of your computer and ensure that the printer you buy is compatible with it. (If the two pieces of equipment do not match up, you will need to buy a further, expensive piece of equipment — an "interface".)

The Program

The final part of the word processor set-up is the most important of all. This is the "software"; the instructions to the computer (which is, of course, the "hardware"), telling it how to process the words. In computer jargon it is called a program (no, that is not mis-spelled) and the program itself is the "word processor". It is a sequence of instructions — in the computer's own language, which you do not need to understand — telling it how to organize your words inside the computer. More important, it will also tell you how to use the program. The better the word-processing program, the easier you, the non-expert, will find it to use. The best word processing programs are what is known as "user friendly" — they tell you what to do next, and offer help on request. (Some computers have a "help" button.)

The best word processors (the programs) display the words all the time on the screen just as they will appear on the paper — sometimes with the one difference that they do not display double-spacing, in order to save screen space. This sort of word processor is known as a "What You See is What You Get" — or WYSIWYG, pronounced "wizziwig" — program. Less convenient for the writer is the other form of display, which deals with the "formatting" of the text as a later, and separate, aspect of the writing process. But this approach to word processing does sometimes — but not always — allow the user to see the layout on the screen after formatting, before printing.

A good word-processor program will allow the user to do many things with the text. Among the more important operations that the program will offer are:

- to insert or delete words, phrases, and even whole paragraphs anywhere within the text, at will;
- to "design" the page at will — to adjust the paragraph indentation for instance, and to change it in the course of a document. (The layout of the typescript of this paragraph was changed: initially the paragraph start was indented; for these itemized points, there is a reversed indent; the initial layout will be reinstated after the last "point".)
- to maintain a continuous word-count throughout a document — and display this count at all times;
- automatically — but under user-control — to divide work up into pages and automatically to insert page numbers at a place on each page decided by the user if wished;
- to "search and replace" or "search and await instruction" — finding

every appearance of a given word which, perhaps, you might wish to change;
- to scroll the typing back to the beginning, or any other point, to permit reading the work through, and editing it at will; and to store the work — and retrieve it reliably.

Not every word-processing program will offer the user all of these facilities — the best offer most.

One set of equipment

It may help readers of this book to investigate the possibilites of word processing for themselves if I describe the equipment that I have invested in — and the problems that I have experienced.

Until Sir Clive Sinclair announced in January 1984 the launch of his new QL computer, I was convinced — possibly wrongly — that I could not afford to set myself up with a word processor. The Sinclair QL however offered a large capacity computer (128K RAM) with a typewriter-like keyboard, its own built-in storage devices capable of storing 100K per cartridge (the Sinclair "Microdrive" cartridges) and a set of four "business user" programs — including a word processor which offered as much as anyone could wish for. So I ordered a QL — by mail order, so I was really buying a pig in a poke — at a cost of £399. Then I scoured the computer magazines for the cheapest prices for monitors (VDUs) and printers. All I knew was that the Sinclair QL would only accept "serial" linkage to a printer.

I identified a Philips green monochrome monitor as being the cheapest and assumed that it could be linked to the QL. The mail-order shop from which I bought it assured me that it could — but at that time almost no one had seen a QL let alone handled one. The monitor cost me just on £80. I discovered that there was a Smith-Corona daisy-wheel printer available with "serial" connections — and that this printer was being discounted very competitively. I bought the Smith-Corona TP–1 printer for £220.

Because, along with other early buyers of the QL, I had to wait so long for delivery, Sinclair Research Ltd. gave me a printer-connector cable — worth about £15. The connection from the QL to the monitor presented rather more problems; no standard cables would fit. Eventually though, the mail-order shop from whom I had bought the monitor made up a cable to special order — cost £7. And with all the bits and pieces plugged together — it still didn't work.

Before the printer would work with the computer it had to be "installed" in the word-processor program. This was simple when I had read the instruction book with great care. The computer can send information to the printer at various speeds — the printer will only accept at one speed and the computer has to be told what this is. This done the whole set-up worked.

I took several hours to read the instruction manual and to experiment with the word processor — I am still discovering new things about it — but effectively, within say 6 hours of successfully joining all the pieces together, I was a user. The whole set-up has cost me just over £700 — including linking cables.

Not all has been straightforward, or perfect with my word processor. There have inevitably been snags. Some of my problems have been due to my inexperience with a computer — I have pressed the wrong button, by accident, and lost a little work; I have neglected to "save" my work ("save", meaning to transfer work from the computer's RAM — which is lost when the power is switched off — to the more permanent storage device, the Microdrive cartridges); and sometimes, even when I have saved it, the storage device has been faulty — and I have lost it anyway.

Some of my problems have been due to the fact that I bought an early production model of the QL. All new machines have minor teething problems — and they get sorted out. (I had to return my initial computer to Sinclair Research — they exchanged it very quickly for a new one.) Other problems have been part of learning to use a new tool. And there has been quite a lot to learn. Again, it may help readers to come more quickly to terms with their word processor/computer if I explain how I — now — work.

Initially, I write onto the screen very quickly. Sometimes I "format" the page before I start writing — this is the "best" way — at other times I merely use what is called the "default" format, that is built into the program. As I write, I keep an eye on the running word-count. (I have a "thing" about the number of words in sentences and paragraphs.) When I have written about 500 words, I save it to the "permanent" store. And I print out a "hard" copy — i.e. a copy on paper — so that whatever happens I have not actually lost my words, even though, in the worst case, I might have to retype them.

Then, often on my daily train journey to work, I read through and correct this first version of my writing. Next time I am working at the keyboard I recall the draft, correct it, and re-save the edited version. At this stage I usually adjust the layout and margins as necessary for the final format before saving. Depending on the length of the work, I then either print it, or make a back-up copy of it, onto another Microdrive cartridge. With these procedures, I feel that I am fairly safe from any electronic loss.

Where I am writing something longer than usual — such as this book chapter — I have learnt, from bitter experience, to save the work piece by piece. This particular chapter was saved as WP1, WP2, WP3, etc., subdividing it at convenient page ends. (Remember, the program shows me — with a line across the screen — just where the page ends are.) Saving like this avoids the potentially damaging process of rewriting over and over again on the same piece of the Microdrive cartridge.

Other set-ups

I can only write from experience about the word processor/computer set-up that I use myself. There are other combinations of home computer, storage device, screen and printer that will do a similar job — but at present, to the best of my knowledge, at greater cost. There are also set-ups that will perhaps be better — but at considerably greater cost.

Some of the other possible systems with an idea of their costs, include:

Amstrad CPC 464 computer, complete with monochrome monitor and built-in cassette storage: £240; 64K RAM; WP program not included but available — on cassette — for about £20; disc drive about £200 extra; printer extra — say £250. Total about £700.

Commodore 64 "Business outfit" computer pack, including computer, dot-matrix printer, disc drive and "Easy-Script" soft-ware: £600; 64K RAM; monitor extra, say £70; daisy-wheel printer an advisable extra, at say £250. Total about £900.

BBC–B computer: £400; 64K RAM: WP program extra — a vast choice, from £10 to £200 — and some available on plug-in ROM ("Read Only Memory") "chips"; disc drive extra, at about £150; monitor extra, at say £70; printer extra, at say £250. Total about £900.

Apricot F1 Personal Computer: £1000; 256K RAM; WP software included in cost; monitor, disc drive and printer are extras — say £70, £200 and £250. Total — for a very superior machine — approximately £1500.

Printers: apart from the Smith-Corona daisy-wheel printer that I bought, the range of daisy-wheels include the Juki 6100 which is a bi-directional printer and costs about £400; the Daisystep 2000 at £280 (both of which are "parallel" operating only) and the Brother HR 15 costing about £380 and available for "serial" or "parallel" operating.

It must be remembered that the equipment mentioned above is a very small selection, almost at random, of the computers and peripheral hardware that is currently available. Many excellent machines are left uncommented on; many more — and probably better — machines will be unveiled before this book is on the bookshelves. My comments on equipment will give you an idea of what to look for; the best thing to do before buying a word processor/computer system is to peruse one of the many personal computer magazines. (The most helpful are probably the weekly *Personal Computer News* and the monthlies *Personal Computer World* and *What Micro*.) And shop around for the best prices — the competition is fierce and the discounting unbelievable.

The Future

As mentioned earlier, the word processor is with us; we must learn to live with it. It will eventually become as essential a part of the writer's equipment as the typewriter is today. Already some, mainly American, book publishers will accept book manuscripts in the form of one or more floppy discs. From these, the publisher's editor can edit directly on screen, the author can check what has been done, and the discs can go directly to the printer; there will be no need for manual typesetting; this will be done by a computer at the printers, working directly from the author's discs. There will be no room for further errors to creep in and — hopefully — no more need for proof-reading.

For the magazine writer the prospect is of being able to work onto the screen and then submit the finished manuscript directly down the telephone line to the screen on the editor's desk. And when an editor wishes to change the text, he will be able to check with the writer, by telephone link from screen to screen. But it will probably still take a long time for the payment cheque to arrive. Computers seem, if anything, to have slowed this part of the process down.

Index of Magazines